TORVILL
AND
DEAN

TORVILL
AND
DEAN

THE FULL STORY

INCLUDING 1994 OLYMPIC DRAMAS

CHRISTOPHER HILTON

The Oxford Illustrated Press

First published in 1994

British Library cataloguing in publication data:
A catalogue record for this book is
available from the British Library

ISBN: 1 85509 238 7

Library of Congress catalog card no. 94-75544

Oxford Illustrated Press is an imprint of Haynes Publishing,
Sparkford, Nr Yeovil, Somerset, BA22 7JJ.

Typeset by G&M, Raunds, Northamptonshire.
Printed in Great Britain by
Butler & Tanner Ltd of London and Frome.

Contents

Acknowledgements

A WORD OF THANKS.

Although this is my personal account of Torvill and Dean's career, I am indebted to them for more than a decade and a half of kindness and courtesy. That applies equally to their coach, Betty Callaway, who invariably helped to set events into context. Nor must I forget the Torvill and Dean families for shared happy times. John Hennessy, who casts a knowing eye over the ice rink for *The Times*, wrote the story of their careers up to 1984 in *Torvill & Dean* (David & Charles, 1984) and I've kept it close to my elbow. Hennessy, a friend, allowed me to use him as a sounding board for this book: a comfort. I reproduce a telling phrase of his with permission. Debbie Turner, who handles Torvill and Dean's publicity, is unfailingly helpful even when faced with the impossible, and Helen Day of Helen Day Promotions leant a hand at a couple of crucial moments. That said, any mistakes in the book are mine. The bulk of the illustrations are from Eileen Langsley of Supersport — my gratitude to her for her care in their selection, and for their scope.

I

Olympic Meltdown

*T*HE PRECISE MOMENT WHEN IT HAPPENED — a corner of a rink at ice-clad Lillehammer, Norway — Torvill and Dean seemed suddenly tired and hollowed. But they stayed true to themselves. They did not sacrifice their dignity. Their stature did not diminish — it grew. He gave a polite wave, she smiled enormously. You would hardly have guessed that the nine cold numerals which had just blinked up on to the big scoreboard ended everything. They were:

5.8　5.7　5.9　5.8　5.7　5.7　5.7　5.6　5.7

These were the marks for technical merit after Jayne Torvill and Christopher Dean skated their free programme, *Let's Face The Music And Dance*, at the Winter

The Winter Olympics, February 1994. They'd faced the music wonderfully and felt sudden, overwhelming relief. Just look at their faces (Supersport).

Olympic Games, February 1994. Any chance of the gold medal had gone. The marks were too low. Jayne held the smile, but Christopher exhaled deeply: a sigh. Within days Torvill and Dean would make a profound decision. They felt they couldn't skate it better and so they retired from amateur competition, missing the World Championships in Tokyo in late March.

Some 23 million televiewers in Britain, virtually half the population — and the second largest BBC audience figure of all time for any programme — saw that sigh at Lillehammer. Many, many people felt enraged by the marks. The 6,000 audience at the rink passed their judgement on the judges by whistling and hooting their derision, but that could not help the quiet couple from Nottingham now. A Russian couple had already had higher marks, and shortly another Russian couple would too. Torvill and Dean finished with bronze. In Britain the sense of outrage was instantaneous, nationwide — and long lasting. A radio station opened a protest phone line

which was immediately blocked with irate callers. In London, sharp front page headlines were being prepared. THE GOLD ROBBERY, END OF AN ICE AGE, GOLD MEDAL ROBBERY.

Torvill and Dean had attempted to defy time. They left competitive skating a full decade earlier, left it with the gold at the 1984 Winter Olympic Games of Sarajevo and echoes of their *Bolero* programme spanning the globe. Their return to temporary 'amateur' status in 1994 following a change in the Olympic rules touched chords far deeper than memory and nostalgia alone could explain. The comeback was fraught with risk and chance — although, as we shall see, risk and chance had governed this golden partnership from its very first moments.

The culmination of their return would be an international furore, with dark tales of conspiracy against them, suggestions that they were punished for having been professionals, accusations of illegal moves during *Let's Face The Music*, the British judge in tears magnified everything enormously, thunderously. In Britain the furore was featured on every television bulletin as a news item of national concern. Within a day, each branch of the media was pumping the controversy hard; 98 per cent of callers to a phone poll insisted Torvill and Dean were robbed.

To understand the furore we must take careful, measured steps. In 1993 the International Skating Union decided to allow professionals to become temporary amateurs. Torvill and Dean regarded this as a challenge, and in January 1994 they won the British Championships at Sheffield with nine perfect marks of 6.0. In a trice the great days seemed to be back. A week and a half later they won the European Championships in Copenhagen, but only through a marking freak. In a trice the great days seemed to have gone again. The judges preferred the fluidity of the Russian couple Maia Usova and Alexandr Zhulin, and preferred the frantic Rock 'n' Roll of the other Russians, Oksana Gritschuk and Evgeny Platov to *Let's Face The Music*.

In secrecy, Torvill and Dean did something they had never done before. Against a time-clock ticking relentlessly, with Lillehammer barely a month off, they accepted that their interpretation of *Let's Face The Music* was too staid, and gutted 80 per cent, replacing this with flamboyance, with showbiz. It piled risk upon risk. Far from honing an established programme they might now have difficulty remembering what to do and when to breathe.

The time-clock ticked so remorselessly that they stayed in Britain working, working, working, and didn't travel to Norway until the first week of the Games. They flew in saying little, but Caroline Searle, spokesperson

The Rhumba, the second section, was a gem of sensuality — opening up, as it seemed, the path to gold (Supersport).

for the team, did say 'they have rooms in a secondary school with a desk, a single bed, and a single wardrobe. It's a bit like a youth hostel'. Vast pressure gathered around them, a frostbite of pressure. Christopher confessed that they had been 'ultra conservative' at Sheffield and Copenhagen, but insisted that remembering the new steps 'keeps our minds active'. It's the way he speaks, and always has.

They unveiled the new version during a practice session. At one point Christopher stumbled, lost the rhythm altogether. Evidently he had gone into a rut left by another couple and it unbalanced him. That aside, the new version lacked the indefinable quality for which they had been famed and fabled — the magic. It looked raw. Nobody had used a word like that about them before, certainly not since they began competing internationally in 1976.

The time ticked. Practice sessions are official and tightly rationed. They could not have the endless hours needed to work and perfect — and also had to think about the other two sections, the compulsory dances on the

The pressure mounted minute by minute and at moments it showed (Supersport).

Friday, and the original dance on the Sunday, before *Let's Face The Music* on the Monday.

The two compulsories, highly technical exercises, were worth only 20 per cent of the total marks, but whoever led after them held a significant advantage. And it went wrong. In the first, the Starlight Waltz, their marks ranged from 5.4 to 5.7, but three judges placed them lower than the relatively obscure Finnish couple Susanna Rahkamo and Petri Kokko, and the Russians were still to come. Torvill and Dean's easy elegance and poise would not be enough. They were third. In the second compulsory, the Blues, their marks ranged from 5.3 to 5.6; the Russians were still to come. The Russians tied, leaving Torvill and Dean still third. The pressure tightened.

Their return had not been universally acclaimed. Stephen Williams, a former ice dancer, said publicly that 'a lot of us couldn't understand why they made the decision to come back. They reached the top, and after that there's only one way, isn't there. If they fail at the Olympics there'll be something to be said'. Many people felt sympathy for Marika Humphreys and Justin Lanning, the defending British champions before Torvill and Dean's comeback, who were now at home watching

Lillehammer on television rather than competing there.

Christopher made astonishing statements after the compulsories. 'It has been harder than we thought, and we were deflated because we skated hard. If we had known before what we know now, we would not have come back because of the mental stress of everything. If someone had given us a glass ball and said *this is what you have got to go through* we wouldn't have done it. We are positive about what we can do, but it's not a question of getting to the line faster than someone else. It's about impressing nine judges and sensing what their general mood is.' They felt resentment did exist, but not against them personally.

'It's just against professionals,' Jayne said. 'It's just a feeling . . .'

'. . . like you shouldn't be here,' Christopher said.

The pressure concentrated on the original dance, worth 30 per cent of the total marks. Each couple skated the Rhumba, but could choose their own music. Torvill and Dean had fashioned a superb and sensuous version of this, performed as slowly as the rules permitted. If they

Let's Face The Music: *a triumph built on a risk, it took the audience by storm and caused a storm* (Supersport).

The podium which enraged Britain. Oksana Gritschuk and Evgeny Platov have gold, Maia Usova and Alexandr Zhulin silver, Torvill and Dean only bronze (Supersport).

did not win this section the gold was essentially gone already. Usova and Zhulin went first of the big three, all softening, snake-like, sinewy motion, and the two sets of marks — composition and presentation — ranged between 5.7 and 5.9. Next came Gritschuk and Platov, she slender and undulating, he sure and strong, but their marks put them below Usova and Zhulin.

As Torvill and Dean waited to come on to the ice Christopher winked at Jayne. It was a jaunty, it'll-be-all-right instant. The 6,000 crowd began clapping before the music started. Torvill and Dean took two or three little breaths and flowed into the Rhumba, haughty, crisp and yet full of caresses, a panorama unfolding.

The Rhumba was a gem. It seized the 6,000 who clapped and cheered as it unfolded, that communal sound-swell which is international and profound. The marks for composition drew a roar:

5.8 5.8 5.9 5.8 5.9 5.9 5.8 5.8 5.9

The marks for presentation drew a bigger roar, deepening into a reverberation, and the great days were back again.

14

5.9 5.9 6.0 5.9 6.0 5.9 5.9 5.9 5.9

Jayne and Christopher embraced, and he said softly 'all right'. It only post-poned the pressure for a heady moment or two. The free programme car-ried 50 per cent of the total marks. Whichever of the big three won that won the gold medal — and the free was tomorrow.

'We were pleased to get that one under the belt,' Christopher said. 'We feel a lot happier than we did two days ago.' Jayne, entirely typically, added 'You could feel the crowd wanting us to skate well. They wanted us to get the marks and we did, so we're pleased'. It's the way she speaks, and always has.

They went through a final practice session next morning, the morning of the free, and as if by a miracle *Let's Face The Music* now looked polished, finished. The stumble of days ago might have been years ago. The draw for order of skating assumed clear importance, because if you are on early the judges have to keep margins for those after you who may skate better. The order was:

Usova and Zhulin
Rahkamo and Kokko
Torvill and Dean
Gritschuk and Platov

Usova and Zhulin wore white and black, but didn't look like dominoes and didn't fall. They were lively, did some jokey trickery and the construction of the programme, its variety, suggested high marks. Technical merit:

5.8 5.8 5.8 5.9 5.8 5.8 5.8 5.8 5.8

The marks for artistic impression narrowed the margins mercilessly.

5.9 5.9 5.8 5.9 5.9 5.9 5.8 5.8 5.9

The Finns did fall, and somehow must have sensed that they were but a prelude. Before they had left the ice, Torvill and Dean came on, he scour-ing his lips with his tongue: nerves? As they circled, loosening and warm-ing themselves — the Finns' marks not yet up — she smiled broadly and raised her eyebrows: nerves? It was a time for that. Would the programme work or collapse? As they settled in mid ice, a little girl — the kind always on hand to gather bouquets — skimmed by to gather one thrown for the Finns. Would the prolonged wait unnerve them? The same thing happened at Sarajevo before *Bolero*.

Let's Face The Music spanned the decade. The crowd was seized again, glo-

rying in the balletic balance of it as well as its ballroom, gorging on the rip-rip-ripple of movement and the enormous finish of a back flip as he flung her over his head. When it was done the crowd were on their feet. Christopher's mouth opened into a very broad grin, he encircled Jayne with his arms, hugging her. She patted his forearm, a homely little gesture of salute and comfort and congratulation.

A few moments later the nine cold numerals held them prisoner. They had lost. To compound that defeat, the Rock 'n' Roll of Gritschuk and Platov took gold, leaving Torvill and Dean with bronze behind Usova and Zhulin. As Torvill and Dean took to the lowest rank on the podium the crowd roared their affection. The furore was poised to break.

Next day Christopher said 'We were a bit confused by the marks. The performance was the best we could have given, and the audience's reaction was our reward. We're glad that we can still be competitive with the other top skaters in the world, we can still measure up 10 years on'. These measured and defensive words did not fuel the furore — but everything else did.

One British newspaper screamed WAS IT RIGGED? The marks provoked that, bringing the pressure now on to the judges. Again we must take careful, measured steps. For technical merit the British judge, Mary Parry, awarded Torvill and Dean 5.9. The Russian and Byelorussian went to 5.8, the Finn, Ukranian, French, Czech and Canadian to 5.7, the German to 5.6. Gritschuk and Platov had two 5.7s, two 5.8s, the rest 5.9s. Usova and Zhulin had eight 5.8s and a 5.9. Why were Torvill and Dean so low? The furore's intensity forced the judges to break their habitual silence.

The Canadian, Jean Senft, said that the back flip had been 'too acrobatic', implying that Christopher's arms were higher than his shoulders as he lifted Jayne: illegal. Senft further said that at one point he had rotated her 'one and a half times in the air': illegal. The German judge, Ingrid Reetz, opted for the vague and the obvious. 'To those in England who are upset by my marking I can only say it was my opinion, honestly given.' The man in charge of the judging, Austrian referee Hans Kutschera, pointed to the back flip, 'an acrobatic movement not allowed under our new rules. They did a kind of jump over the head, and for this fault they lost marks'. Under pressure to comment on whether there had been a conspiracy against Torvill and Dean he opted for these words: 'My sport is OK'.

Of the back flip Christopher explained that 'it's to do with lifting the lady above your shoulders, but at the point when Jayne goes over my head

it's all inertia. I initiate her from my body, from my hips. I push back, which sends her into the air, and all that happens is she's pivoting around my hands. I'm not holding her or lifting her in any way, so it's effectively a jump by herself at that time'.

Had such a furore ever been stirred anywhere, any time, by the arrangement of two human bodies for one milli-second in time?

On top of the 5.9 for technical merit, Mary Parry had given Torvill and Dean 6.0 for artistic impression, and was the only judge to place them first overall. Kutschera ordered her to give a written explanation and she burst into tears. 'They won't allow me to say anything,' she said, 'but he has rather upset me, and I have to stand up and be counted. There are obviously going to be questions asked. To me, Torvill and Dean's programme was *the* programme. Everyone is going to look at this and say "What's going on?" It's not helped the sport at all. I was not surprised I was out on a limb. I expected to be.'

Torvill and Dean maintained their dignity and stature. The reception from the crowd, he said, had been their gold medal.

That day he announced his engagement to his fiancée Jill Trenary, a former United States world champion skater. Shortly after the free dance he had made the proper gesture and got down on one knee to propose. She found that 'kinda cute'.

Juan Antonio Samaranch, President of the International Olympic Committee, did not find the events surrounding the ice dancing cute at all and made threatening noises that if the marking wasn't sorted out, ice dancing might no longer be an Olympic sport.

Under this pressure Kutschera called a Press Conference, something unique. He reiterated that Torvill and Dean's back flip was illegal but reportedly 'blustered and bellowed' trying to defend his panel's decision to give them bronze. Moreover, to clear evidence that Gritschuk and Platov had 'separated' during their programme — skated apart, in fact — for more than the permitted five seconds, Kutschera would say not one word. Someone timed the separation at 13 seconds . . .

Why mark one couple down and not the other?

Lawrence Demmy, vice-president of the ISU, now went public. 'They — Torvill and Dean — got a medal but in my opinion it was the wrong colour. Torvill and Dean should have won because they were the best.' Demmy accepted illegalities in their routine but pointed to *two* separations by the Russians of over five seconds. 'I can only assume that the judges were

LEFT The intimacy of Bolero *hadn't been diluted by time* (Supersport).

ABOVE This is what the crowd thought of Bolero — *and what they thought of Torvill and Dean. Simply the best, better than all the rest* (Supersport).

not precisely aware of the duration of the separations. That does not concern me. The penalties should have balanced out.'

Mary Parry returned to Britain and gave an interview to BBC Radio Leeds (paradoxically I was on the same programme but didn't have the chance to question her myself). She mounted a resolute defence of her marks, albeit within the confines of what she *could* say. Judges don't exactly take a vow of silence — but almost.

'I cannot answer for the other judges', she said, 'What I did was the way I saw it. I was a little surprised they were marked so low for technical merit.' The back flip? 'As far as I am concerned it is not illegal. Jayne jumps, she is not lifted. And Torvill and Dean must know the rules. That is correct, that is absolutely right.'

She said she'd sensed that a 'slight feeling' of resentment existed at the Europeans about professionals coming back but at the Olmpics 'definitely not'. Overall, she concluded, she had nothing to be ashamed of. 'I kept my head up.'

Would Torvill and Dean go on to the Worlds in Japan? After

The Winter Olympics had private as well as public perspectives. Dean announced his engagement to Jill Trenary (Press Association).

Lillehammer they spoke of the mental and physical strain again, and somehow it showed. They made an announcement 10 days after the free programme.

'The Olympics was such a big high for us,' Christopher said, 'and it was a performance we don't think we'll ever be able to repeat, under those circumstances in competition. It just seemed a great point to say "OK, this is it". We feel that the audience on the day around the world were our judges. The World Championships were in our game plan but we felt we'd done the best we could and we felt the die had been cast a little bit.'

It was the nearest he'd come to provoking controversy himself. He'd always been like that: let others express heated opinions. Jayne sat beside him smiling, which she'd always done. They'd matured over the years but remained essentially the people they were when they began.

2

From Copper to Gold

S TRASBOURG, A CROSSROADS OF A CITY, was the right place to hold the European Skating Championships. The architecture was German, the decor and food French, the language a patois between Deutsch and Français. A host of Common Market institutions regarded it as home. Someone mentioned casually that the British team contained a policeman. Pardon? Yes, no mistake, he's a policeman and he's an ice dancer. He's from Nottingham and so is his partner. Skating conjured many images — feline grace and sequins and the rest, *but not a bobby on the beat.*

It was February 1978.

I went looking and found him in a corridor of the official hotel. That first impression: a tall, blond, clean-cut young man who can scarcely have been interviewed before. He stood erect, as the constabulary demands, and diffident. It was natural to assume that a policeman's reticence held him, as if he feared anything said might be taken down and used in evidence. Only later did it emerge that the diffidence was straightforward shyness, itself a paradox in a policeman, never mind a performing policeman.

Quietly, his voice nearly a whisper, he charted his life in Nottingham. He said how he tried to balance the skating with his duties and sometimes it was hard 'to grab a meal'. If he worked the night shift he and his partner had to go to the rink at dawn to practise, but, he said, if you want something in life you go out and do it. He worried that because the balancing of two lives made him tired he was more vulnerable to colds.

Natural sentiments for a 19-year-old. In Strasbourg Robin Cousins represented the big story as he moved, step by step, on the long journey towards the Winter Olympics in 1980 where he intended to follow John Curry who'd won gold in 1976. Christopher Dean was just another member of the British team, as anonymous as his partner Jayne Torvill. They finished ninth at Strasbourg. Not at all bad but the probability was that in time, like many a dozen others, they'd simply melt away — a cameo of a career which went so far and no further.

He'd concentrate on arresting felons in Nottingham and he'd give you

examples. One Saturday a drunk undressed in the street and Dean bundled him smartly into a Black Maria. He chased another and received a whack in the mouth for his trouble. No doubt Dean would rise within the police if he matured out of the shyness. He looked the kind — intelligent, calm, responsible.

Torvill, equally, would concentrate on her job as an insurance clerk in the Norwich Union (where, rumour insisted, she was famous for unpunctuality). She'd left school at 16 with a couple of 'O' levels. Now, in 1978, she and Dean were a handsome couple although not contemplating marriage. They'd been in love, or rather thought they were in love but sensed they were too young to really know. It's a brave and sensible judgement if only because most teenagers don't reason like that. Whatever, the love had melted, the way it can. It gave them, however, two strengths — they were accustomed to touch, and on the ice they could re-create the intimacy of lovers and never seem to be feigning it.

Probably no-one but Torvill and Dean and their first trainer, Janet Sawbridge, had seen their qualities and their potential, or the foundation on which it was built. They came from solid stock and dealt in common-sense rather than flights of fancy: Christopher's father was a mining engineer, and his step-mother a homely woman; Jayne's parents ran a corner shop. Such folk have backbone and form the backbone of a country. Torvill and Dean inherited much, not least a doggedness in pursuit of what they wanted to do.

How they got as far as Strasbourg was riven with chance and improbability.

Jayne Torvill, born in Nottingham on 7 October 1957, started skating at nine. She went because the teacher at school decided to organise a trip to the rink on a Friday evening. 'I went the first week and thought it was great. I went the second week and passed a certificate to say I could skate forwards and backwards.' Picture the tiny elf of a girl exploring the wonders of movement on ice and picture also her method of making sure her parents couldn't get her off it to take her home. She moved to the middle of the rink and stayed there beyond reach.

It's the way you begin, the way everybody begins: go along, hire skates (which can be stiff and unyielding), step gingerly out. Initially ice seems very, very slippery and a rink spreads itself broad and intimidating unless you have a natural ability to stand up on the ice. If you do it's wonderful, a rediscovering of motion. The nine-year-old has advantages, lightness, bones not yet brittle — and nine-year-olds are impudent of risk anyway. At virtually any rink you see first-time adults clinging to the sides or making nervous waddling motions near the sides while hordes of kids whizz by, easy as you like, fashioning pirouettes and spins.

Jayne says she 'pestered my mum and dad like mad. "Please take me skating on Saturday. I can't skate in those hired boots. *Please* will you buy me some?"' Her parents assumed this was a passing phase but did buy her a second-hand pair and 'I had those for a whole year'.

She progressed along the orthodox route as a solo skater and then joined another Nottingham skater, Michael Hutchinson, to compete as a pair. Pairs skating is separate from ice dancing, less artistic and more regimented, with prescribed lifts and throws.

Torvill and Hutchinson made a handy partnership. In 1970 they won the British junior title and came second in the seniors, won the seniors the following year but were beaten the year after that, when they finished eighteenth in the European Championship. It melted. Hutchinson departed for London to find a new partner. Jayne returned to solo skating and continued for the love of it.

Christopher Dean, born in Nottingham on 27 July 1958, started skating

The bobby on the beat, shy but helpful and looking very much the part (Nottingham Evening Post).

aged 10. The family lived outside Nottingham and his parents suggested he took up a sport because he'd always played at school and it would give him 'an outside interest' rather than let the claustrophobia of their small village envelop him. 'I went down and had a look and said "OK, I'll try it". I got a pair of skates for Christmas and the following week I started. I was on my backside more than my feet.' He'd remember that first impression: black and blue.

Christopher's father Colin would assess his son as 'always quite shy and rather withdrawn. It could have been interpreted as standoffishness. He took schooling seriously and was average in the classroom. We talked about quite a few different things for him to do, even ballroom dancing. We bought him skates for £15 but it was up to him whether he liked it or not'.

He and they travelled to Nottingham Stadium, the city's rink — where Jayne had begun — and were asked what kind of lessons they'd like for Christopher, solo, pairs or dancing? In a fateful moment they chose the last because they enjoyed dancing themselves. It was as simple as that.

After two years Christopher progressed to the point where he needed a regular partner and found one in Sandra Elson, a girl already ice dancing at

the rink. 'Our parents,' she remembers, 'talked about it in the restaurant at Nottingham Stadium. He had style on the ice and people said we had potential.' They also had temperaments and tempers and 'bickered' on the ice. Despite that they won the British primary championships in 1972 while Jayne, who Christopher knew only to look at, skated pairs with Hutchinson.

Elson and Dean, trained by a man called Len Sayward, won the British Juniors in 1974 and came sixth in the seniors. When Sayward was offered a job at Grimsby, Elson thought they ought to follow him there. Dean, now a police cadet, said no. More bickering. Nottingham hired Janet Sawbridge — British ice dance champion three times, the last in 1971 — to replace Sayward and she inherited Elson and Dean. Within a few days Sawbridge witnessed the final explosion. Dean stormed off the ice one way, Elson the other and they never did get back on

BELOW LEFT Who could know that in time the bobby on the beat would look like this? (Supersport).

BELOW RIGHT They move towards second place in the Rotary Watches competition at Richmond, Surrey, in 1979 (Colorsport).

Who could know that the bobby on the beat would create a vision of heaven looking like this? (Supersport).

it together. Years later Elson would confide that 'then came the rift and I got another partner, an absolute mistake'.

The world would never know Elson and Dean and scarcely remember Torvill and Hutchinson.

Sawbridge cast around for a new partner, trawling laboriously through the National Skating Association handbook which listed everyone of the right standard. She found three names but two had partners and, worse, lived in Birmingham and London, an insuperable barrier to sustained, regular training. Moreover one of the two seemed to have a temperament akin to Ms Elson and Sawbridge wanted no more explosions, thank you. The third name genuinely surprised Sawbridge because she was already teaching her as a solo skater. Jayne Torvill. Evidently Torvill had done a bit of ice dancing years before and been competent enough to have it recorded in the handbook.

Sawbridge said to Christopher *We've somebody in our own rink. What do you think?* They concluded that they had nothing to lose. It was May 1975. Sawbridge left Christopher at the rinkside and walked to the ladies changing room. She asked Jayne if she was prepared to have a trial with

Christopher and remembers Jayne as 'shocked. She really didn't give me an answer'. Sawbridge took that as affirmative, returned to the rinkside and waited for Jayne to come along.

(Thereby hangs a tale. Many years later, when I'd interviewed Sawbridge about this, I played the tape to Torvill and Dean because they were extremely curious about what she'd said. They chuckled through the chance and improbability of it except for one moment. Sawbridge seemed to remember her initial approach to Jayne had been when Torvill was in the loo, the conversation being conducted under the door. Jayne was sure it hadn't been, but chortled as she denied it.)

Jayne did come along, they chatted and agreed they'd give it a try for a month. They didn't want to pledge any longer than that because, Christopher says, 'we both knew that if you commit yourself things go wrong, so we didn't say we were partners'. (Later, when Sawbridge pressed them for a decision, their superstitions — and both are superstitious — impelled them to leave the arrangement as it was, murmuring only 'well, we'll give it another month'. They maintained this long after the decision had been made.)

Ice rinks are commercial enterprises open to the paying public. This is how Jayne and Christopher took it up, but inevitably it militates against competition skaters who need clear ice, time of their own and a calm for concentration. They go outside the public sessions and every British competitor has suffered the dawn run and the late night slog stretching beyond midnight.

At six o'clock the morning after Sawbridge's approach and the rinkside chat, Nottingham Stadium — an echoing, sombre edifice of a place — was largely deserted as they moved onto the ice to explore their potential together, see if they could create a partnership.

Sawbridge remembers that initial impression, remembers their fragility, how 'one was a bit scared to hold the other'. Both needed to adjust because Elson had stood virtually the same height as Christopher, 5ft 1oin, while Jayne stood only 5ft and a precious half inch. He'd have to compensate for that and so would Jayne — by definition ice dancers cannot look ungainly. They chugged around a bit experimenting with simple turns and didn't dare venture proper dance steps, but Sawbridge, shrewd, noticed how they immediately looked 'nice' — the dark hair against the blond, the short somehow complementing the tall. The 'commanding man' was already there in Christopher.

Jayne remembers the next night when they did venture a bit of dancing. She coins a hard word to describe it. 'Ghastly.' She fell, giving her elbow

and head a smart thump. In the background many watched critically. The competitors at any rink are a small community monitoring each other, gossiping, charting move and counter-move within the community. She knew what some thought: Torvill and Dean are a forced mis-match, they're the wrong sizes for each other and she's barely been an ice dancer. She'd remember someone telling Christopher what a howler he'd made with this little Torvill. She'd never forget that.

Perhaps something more than exploration was born that evening. If those of a critical nature insisted on a mis-match, Torvill and Dean would be dogged and show them; and if anything on earth would make Jayne Torvill get up and do it again and again, it was a fall and a thump.

They moulded to each other quickly and soon enough needed to pass a test called the Inter-gold in order to take part in the British Championships. The test went like this: They skated to a piece of music and the judges marked the man, then they repeated it to the same piece of music and the judges marked the woman. It didn't go well the first time. In fact it went so badly that there was a risk that Christopher would destroy Jayne's marks when they skated the second time. They walked along the rinkside with Sawbridge urging Christopher to do it, *do it for Jayne,* and he did, skated 'like he'd never done before'. In context it was their first great performance.

At that moment Janet Sawbridge mused that they shouldn't really worry about the British Championships; no, they should be thinking about the world . . .

The Deans moved into Nottingham to within walking distance of where Jayne lived above the corner shop — a bell that trilled when you opened the door; newspapers, magazines, confectionery. In the years to come George and Betty Torvill would gaze down at their own counter and see some wondrous headlines about their daughter who, even when great fame had overtaken her, liked to put on a smock and serve, or have a nap on the sofa in the back room. Yes, solid stock, feet on *terra firma*.

The Deans' move simplified the logistics of training because, as the partnership bonded and improved, the training increased. The hours of training, dawn run or night slog, isolated them from the habits and habitats of ordinary young people, drawing them even closer.

It's a delicate bloom, this process, and incentives help enormously because they act as propulsion, dispelling such nagging notions as whether you're wasting your time. In 1976, their first season, they won a couple of minor championships, one called the Sheffield Trophy, the other called the Northern. That opened up selection by the National Skating Association to

go to summer competitions in St. Gervais, France and Oberstdorf, Bavaria.

That drew them closer still. They were beaten at Oberstdorf only by a Soviet couple, Marina Zueva and Andrei Vitman, won St. Gervais — the Soviets didn't go there — and that autumn came fourth in the British Championships, then traditionally held at Nottingham. They had propulsion, but how far would it propel them, or more properly how far would they propel it?

Christopher records how, as part of his probationary training in the police, he was dispatched to Dishforth, Yorkshire, for 10 long, awkward weeks. He'd journey back on a Friday to Nottingham where Jayne had been waiting all week. Being an insurance clerk represented good employment but not real fulfilment for a lively, talented young lady with the world to beat. Mid-week she spent time on the ice by herself, no doubt rehearsing moves as best she could.

Those weekends he'd immediately join her at the Stadium and they wouldn't waste a minute until he had to return to Dishforth. But it proved

ABOVE LEFT The mentor, advisor and pillar of strength. Betty Callaway with her smile — but look at the eyes. They drove a Soviet camera crew off (Supersport).

ABOVE RIGHT In competitive ice dancing you find slots to occupy and then move up. Torvill and Dean finding their slot — fourth — in the 1980 European Championships in Gothenburg (Colorsport).

hard discipline — he exhausted by the week's exertions as a cadet, she impatient to practice, work, practice, work. Christopher attributes the survival of the partnership to her determination. *OK, we're separated and we can't work, practice, work, practice as we want and need, but if she won't give up I won't give up.*

In retrospect, the notion of giving up appears an absurdity, a violation of nature. It did not seem so in the summer of 1977. Christopher saw the rest of his life as a policeman and the skating as something else he could do — and do well, but with a time-limit hanging over it. One of these days he and she would stop, would concentrate on their real jobs the way moderately successful sportspeople do. Melt away, in fact.

In the autumn of 1977 they came third in the British Championships, earning a place in the British team for the European Championships in Strasbourg and the World Championships in Ottawa. A bobby on the beat? Yes, no mistake, he's a policeman and he's an ice dancer. He's from Nottingham and so is his partner.

Now that Torvill and Dean have reached international

The Original Set Pattern dance at Gothenburg, the facial gestures already radiating confidence and pleasure (Colorsport).

status, we need to pause to examine the structure of a skating season because it makes the narrative easier to comprehend and carries an importance of its own; and this importance will magnify as Torvill and Dean grow in stature.

Speed, poise and a little showmanship at Gothenburg – and Christopher lived on boiled rice and black tea (Colorsport).

The British Ice Dance Championships were held at Nottingham in late November. The European Championships followed in January, and the Worlds in March with, every four years, the Winter Olympics in February.

It was a cyclical season, giving skaters the summer to prepare. The Britons would unveil their programmes at the British and hone them through the Europeans, Olympics (should it be an Olympic year) and Worlds with virtually no chance to make fundamental alterations. The Championships chased each other too fast, the risk of major surgery, particularly on the important free dance — requiring dozens and dozens of hours to bring to fruition — would be too great.

The British Championships were pivotal. Do well there and you'd made a platform for the season. Do badly and every continental judge — skating has a merciless grapevine — would know and draw appropriate conclusions. We'll come to the intrigue, politics and mysteries of international judging in good time. Suffice it to say here that if you blew it at Nottingham your chances of significant improvement in your finishing place in the Europeans became minimal and that continued like a ripple through the Olympics and Worlds. We'll also come to how a competition works, section by section; again suffice it to say here that the free dance — a couple's own creation and carrying most marks — was of great importance to their fate.

On the way up in skating you seek to establish slots. Ice dancers do not arrive from nowhere and storm championships at the first time of asking. They serve an apprenticeship, establishing a lowly slot with the clear aim of moving up to another slot the next season and so on until they either run out of propulsion or find themselves amongst the podiums and medals. It can take a long time to reach there and would occupy Torvill and Dean for four years.

They established an initial slot at the 1978 Europeans at Strasbourg — ninth — moved steadily up for the next two seasons, and only then plundered everything.

At Strasbourg their free programme — she in light green, he in dark green — looked heavily rehearsed, the hand gesturing calculated and formal. They pursued the music rather than manipulating the music to what they wanted it to be. Christopher confesses that afterwards he could remember virtually nothing of it and Jayne explains why. 'We were so scared. It's such a big thing at the time and as long as you start and finish that's all that matters. It's a question of getting through it.'

The free dance did contain tantalizing glimpses to anyone looking closely. Torvill and Dean showed a visible competence, and they concealed their anxiety by doing what you have to do: smile, smile, smile. And, however taught and rehearsed the gestures, they brought to these a flourish: Here, look at this! They drew deep applause from the audience, no matter that they were feeling their way towards a slot. They behaved like learners learning. They watched what the big names did, saw how the big names behaved, monitored how the big names approached it.

In particular Jayne spotted a Hungarian couple, Krisztina Regoeczy and Andras Sallay. She noted how before they skated they held hands in the most relaxed

RIGHT The 1980 World Championships at Dortmund, and they handle the Starlight Waltz crisply (Wilfried Witters).

34

ABOVE LEFT *In 1981 Torvill and Dean began to win their cold war against the Soviets, although it would last until 1984. Marina Klimova and Sergei Ponomarenko had grace* (Supersport).

ABOVE RIGHT *Klimova and Ponomarenko could create magical, feline moments* (Supersport).

way and he gave her a peck of a kiss immediately before they went on. Jayne had anticipated that the couples at Strasbourg would be 'aggressive and competitive' which of course they were. But the Hungarians showed you could approach that in the way suiting you.

It's a powerful lesson: *Be strong enough to be yourself.* Like the insult when she joined Christopher in the first place, she would not forget. Neither would he.

Janet Sawbridge, by now married and pregnant, travelled to Strasbourg, but clearly in the immediate future her time would have to be channelled towards her family, a natural question of priorities. Perhaps history has given her less than her due, because what she did was drowned by so much deepening, echoing applause long after she'd departed. But she brought Torvill and Dean together, handled their most sensitive years — not just the exploration but the possibility of self-doubts — and between 1975 and 1978 helped them from the stage when Jayne was banging her head and elbow to a very respectable slot in the European Championships. At one point she waived her tuition fees altogether.

Now, however, other priorities pressed down on her. She could manage only a single lesson between Strasbourg and the World Championships in Ottawa — but chance and improbability played their hand again, in the Canadian capital. Christopher was in the lift at the team's hotel and in stepped an externally austere, slightly forbidding English lady. Her interest in these 1978 World Championships centred on Regoeczy and Sallay, whom she trained.

She was called Betty Callaway.

Callaway remembered Torvill and Dean from Strasbourg, remembered thinking they 'looked quite interesting and really thought no more about it'. In the lift she recognised Christopher, knew somehow he'd been suffering from a cold and said 'Oh, hello, I've heard you've been ill. How are you? Do you feel better?' He was so painfully shy he just about managed to say 'Yes, thank you'. He'd never use four words when two would do. In this case, and under duress, he managed three.

Torvill and Dean finished eleventh, disappointing

The powerhouse from Moscow, Natalia Bestemianova and Andrei Bukin, strong as the wind off the Steppes (Supersport).

because others who might have been in lower slots moved to higher slots. On the last night, after the free dance, 'I found a dress hanging up,' Callaway says. 'I remembered the colour and wondered if it was the little British girl's dress so I took it back to the hotel and it was Jayne's.' Jayne, evidently, had forgotten it — legend relates that it was draped over a dustbin. Whatever, contact had been made. It would actively last for more than 15 years.

Torvill and Dean returned to Nottingham and, visiting Janet Sawbridge in the maternity unit, were relieved when she said she intended to stop coaching. They sensed they'd already moved beyond anything but total commitment and, despite the gratitude they felt towards her — and they did — they felt that the weight of her priorities would not permit her to give them what they now required.

They sought guidance from the manager of Nottingham Stadium, Roy Sanders. He contacted Betty Callaway. Chance and improbability played their hand again. Regoeczy and Sallay had written from Budapest and as Callaway read the letter she understood that they had retired. She would not have countenanced taking on another couple otherwise.

She travelled to Nottingham one Thursday. They met in the cafeteria — a modest place, as you'd anticipate, formica and tin trays and plain English grub — and talked it over. Jointly they agreed, in what ought now to be a time-honoured phrase, to 'give it a month's trial'.

During the meeting Callaway cast a penetrating eye on Jayne and Christopher, assessing them as people rather than skaters. The bond between a coach and her couple is so personal — an interlocking of destinies and those dozens and dozens of hours of grind, perhaps some discipline, hard words, mutual respect — that it is axiomatic that all three partners should actually like each other. She distills this. 'I always knew that they had something special but you have to become good friends and you have to become close.'

The Regoeczy-Sallay retirement proved a complete misunderstanding, Callaway not properly grasping a phrase in their letter. She now had two couples.

She and the Hungarians regularly travelled to Nottingham at weekends and both couples trained together. 'It helped a lot having Andras that first year because they all became really good pals, and of course Andras and Krisztina were very polished. Some of that rubbed off. Christopher and Jayne were still very shy but dedicated and knew what they wanted to do. They are also very astute. They learnt by watching. Gradually you could see it coming through.'

In a personal town-twinning, Torvill and Dean would also train in

Budapest. 'Andras had a ballet teacher,' Callaway says, 'a great character and a real man and Christopher learnt that you don't have to look sissy to show your emotions and your feelings on the ice. We went to Budapest because of the facilities there and also I reasoned that if Christopher and Jayne were going to be brought out as people we needed to travel and meet more situations.

'In some ways a policeman does keep a certain distance from everybody and being a policeman held him back at the beginning. He was so fair-haired and a little bit nervous at the Championships that he used to look as if he'd peg out on us, so we insisted that he put some colour on his face — but we literally had to sit on him. Krisztina, Krisztina's mother, the British team leader: we literally held him down to put it on. Of course he soon realised the importance and the ballet teacher helped enormously.'

BELOW LEFT In time, and in Torvill and Dean's wake, Bestemianova and Bukin wouldn't be afraid of the spectacular (Supersport).

BELOW RIGHT Nor would Bestemianova and Bukin be afraid of showing their full range of emotions (Supersport).

It must be said that Christopher's fellow police officers occasionally stopped by Nottingham Stadium to have a giggle at this ice dancing-prancing *and stayed to watch.*

Meanwhile Callaway, long experienced, worked to a precise formula. She never scolded or administered reprimands, she encouraged them to explore their own abilities. She issued no orders but firmly requested them to examine and dissect for themselves what they were doing, why it worked or didn't work. This is a mature formula as well as a sympathetic one. It allows a couple the space to mature in their own way, broaden their exploration. Callaway is guide and coach. No doubt early on she grasped something significant: Jayne and Christopher would carve a lot of space and fill it in their own way.

She kept to herself, however, the right to culminate training sessions when to prolong them was futile or counter-productive. Jayne and Christopher displayed a hunger for practice which repetition could not dull — Christopher, defensively, would say 'we never actually get to the point of saying "oh, no, not skating again" because if you did you'd have to get out'. Callaway announced the point of no return in a session with the words *well, that's enough.* They obeyed, however much the hunger invited them to skate and re-skate and re-skate a particular movement until they could do it safely, endlessly and precisely as they wanted to.

Callaway accepted, as Elson and Sawbridge had discovered, that Christopher could be explosive, particularly if what he considered perfection eluded him on any particular day. She allowed the explosions to detonate and subside, might occasionally thrust in a stern word or two of her own but all three understood that when the subsiding had been completed the 'incident' which provoked the explosion died with it: did not linger after they came off the ice and certainly did not fester.

In her pragmatic fashion Callaway felt the explosions might be A Good Thing. She had artistry on her hands and what real artist lacks temperament? One measure of Christopher was, and is, that at pressure moments he exercised merciless self control, willed himself to be completely calm. Volcanic skaters who don't are better advised to try some other sport.

They won the 1978 British Championships and were awarded their first 6.0, although as John Hennessy, an early biographer, points out it came from a judge fabled for generosity and therefore wasn't taken as a shaft of light. More revealingly, they drew 5.8 and 5.9 from Courtney Jones, a former World Champion who at that time refused on principle ever to bestow the ultimate mark, the 6.0. Going towards the 1979 European Championships in Zagreb in January it was time to move up some international slots.

We need to pause here again to examine the structure of competition. The championships were skated in three self-contained sections: three compulsory dances, an original set pattern, and the free dance. Don't be daunted. It has a logic and a simplicity and, if you're new to it, a surprise. Let's look at the surprise. Nine judges awarded marks but these marks — the ones you see springing up in a row on scoreboards — were not ends in themselves. They showed how each judge evaluated a couple against all the other couples.

A great moment. Torvill and Dean prepare to start their first compulsory dance, the Westminster Waltz, at the 1981 European Championships, Innsbruck (Colorsport).

The winner of the competition was the couple who secured a majority of first places from the judges. Thus if a judge marked a couple as low as, say, 5.5, that didn't kill the couple's chances provided the judge marked all the others below 5.5. The couple had won a judge. If, overall, the couple won at least five of the nine judges they held a winning majority. In the event of a tie-break it moved to the judges' choice of second places. (This could produce, in extremis, bizarre results. It climaxed during the 1994 European Championships in Copenhagen, bringing Torvill and Dean to victory when, superficially, they lay third.) The marks are the only way judges

LEFT The dignity of the Waltz, all crisp, clean control (Colorsport).

can show who they've put in the lead, who in second place, third and so on.

Now for the three self-contained sections:

The *compulsories* (officially known as the Prescribed Pattern Dances) were announced by the International Skating Union a year in advance to give couples ample time to practice them. The compulsories were then the same for national and international competitions. What you skated at Nottingham you'd be skating again in Zagreb and the Worlds in Vienna. In 1979 they were the Viennese Waltz, the Yankee Polka and the Blues. Each dance was marked after it had been skated, giving couples three sets of marks. The compulsories, a test of technique, positioning, timing and precision, were worth 30 per cent of the whole competition.

The *original set pattern* (popularly abbreviated to the OSP) was also announced a year in advance. The International Skating Union chose the tempo but couples had more freedom of expression in what they did with it. In 1979 the OSP was the waltz. It carried two sets of marks, for composition and presentation, and was worth 20 per cent of the whole competition.

The *free dance* was a programme of four minutes and the couple's own choice. All they had to do was stay within the rules governing the kind of movements they could make and use music acceptable for dancing, no vocals permitted. The free carried two sets of marks, for technical merit and artistic impression. The free was worth 50 per cent of the whole competition.

In Zagreb in 1979, Torvill and Dean faced not only Regoeczy and Sallay but also the leading exponents of ice dancing, two Soviet couples: Natalia Linichuk and Gennadi Karponosov, and Irina Moiseeva — face like a Tzarina, the eyes all power and mystery and snow off the Steppes — and Andrei Minenkov (dubbed Min and Mo by the Brits, which they didn't like). To demonstrate the standards and how many slots Torvill and Dean would need to move up eventually, here are the marks for the Viennese Waltz:

Linichuk, Karponosov

5.6 5.5 5.6 5.6 5.6 5.5 5.6 5.5 5.6

Torvill, Dean

4.8 4.9 4.8 4.7 4.8 4.8 5.1 5.0 4.9

To demonstrate judging in action, here are the positions the judges placed them in after the three compulsories:

Linichuk, Karponosov

1   1   1   1   1   1   1   1   1

Torvill, Dean

6   7   6   7   5   6   5   5   5

Incidentally, because the compulsories were so technical the marks habitually fell far, far below the maximum 6.0. Please remember that.

Zagreb in winter: a soiled sort of a city, quasi-communist, cracked pavements and glistening, muddy pot holes in the roads, a web of industry, workers' apartment blocks standing like sentries to a creed, taxi drivers you couldn't trust. (I got done from the railway station to the hotel and I'm still looking for the driver. He knew I didn't know about dinars.)

Never mind, in cities where not much is going on the locals flock to the rink with its bright lights and promise of delights, and they flocked. They saw Linichuk and Karponosov win the European Championships, Torvill and Dean feeling their way into sixth slot. In view of what was so imminent (on an ice dancing time scale) it's worth setting out the comparative artistic impression marks in the free dance:

Linichuk, Karponosov

5.8   5.9   5.9   5.9   5.9   5.9   5.9   5.9   5.9

Torvill, Dean

5.3   5.5   5.2   5.3   5.3   5.3   5.6   5.4   5.3

They moved down to eighth in the 1979 Worlds when the North Americans came in, then trained hard across the summer in preparation for 1980, an Olympic year. They won the 1979 British Championships but, of much more significance, finished second in the prestigious NHK competition in Tokyo, nearly beating Min and Mo. Judges give credence to that, draw their appropriate conclusions. By now, too, still balancing their careers with the skating, they'd begun the maturing as people: and maturity is valuable in ice dancing. Teenagers may seize solo skating events but not dancing.

Torvill and Dean flowed and bubbled. They'd mastered it to the extent where they could radiate their own pleasure rather than be haunted by making mistakes, and that communicated itself. At the 1980 European Championships in Gothenburg they finished fourth, even though Christopher had a queasy stomach and survived on boiled rice and black tea during the run-up. He lost so much weight Jayne thought he looked

Harmony of movement in the Waltz, Jayne having the time of her life and showing it (Colorsport).

'skinny' and doubtless told him so, her face full of mischief.

The Winter Olympics were at Lake Placid, a completely absurd place to hold anything bigger than a whist drive. The full majesty and scale of an Olympic Games descended upon a hapless hamlet in Upstate New York with virtually no roads, no amenities and the local vicar himself heading the organising committee.

Many are the tales told. Two will do, because I don't want to be more vindictive than is necessary.

Reportedly at one medal ceremony, held on frozen Lake Placid itself, only two of the three medal winners had been informed of the arrangements, leaving one vacant place on the podium. Someone dropped the gold medal into the snow before it had been presented, and while Very Important People scrabbled around trying to find it they heard the distinctive sound of cracking ice . . .

Transport, crucial to moving officials, competitors and spectators to make the Games function, lay largely in the province of Canadian school buses brought down over the border. Reportedly (who knew truth in the midst of all this?) the drivers heard that the few American drivers were being paid more so withdrew themselves, their labour and their buses back over the border.

The Governor of New York declared a state of emergency, giving him martial powers, and ordered bus companies to *send what you have now, this minute*. One night the road to Lake Placid began to tremble under the weight of them, some from as far afield as New Jersey, and barely a driver with a notion of where to report. We went to bed with Main Street empty and awoke to find it packed solid.

Christopher remembers the chaos. He and Jayne flew to Montreal and had a three hour bus journey to the Olympic Village — which in ordinary life was a prison. They waited outside for 'about two hours' to get their accreditation and when they went in were amazed (that's being diplomatic) 'how small the rooms were. You couldn't swing a cat and we had two people in these rooms'.

Jayne, sharing with another ice dancer, Karen Barber, had a tactical talk. They devoted a couple of hours to adjusting the furniture this way and that to make the room bigger or at least make it seem bigger but it stubbornly remained the same size when they'd finished.

None could escape further chaos at the opening ceremony. This was usually a warm-hearted and emotional gathering of the world's youth. They enter a vast arena, country by country in alphabetical order, forming up in the middle to await the arrival of a runner bearing a torch — brought in

relays from Greece — who ascends steps and lights the Olympic flame. It was cold that ice-clad afternoon, a dry, stinging, frightening cold. The ceremony dragged on so long that the cold struck at Jayne and she began to cry. Her hands went completely numb and the nightmarish thought of frostbite reared. With the ceremony mercifully over, they boarded an overheated bus to return to the Village and, thawing out, her hands hurt again.

They were lucky. In general the transport failed and the torch-bearer, in singlet and vest, could not find a bus and tramped towards Lake Placid getting very strange looks.

ABOVE LEFT Another great moment. Torvill and Dean lock into their starting position for the crucial free dance at Innsbruck (Colorsport).

ABOVE RIGHT The free dance, skated to four interwoven pieces of music, gave hints of the glories that lay not far ahead (Colorsport).

The British media concentrated on Robin Cousins. He duly delivered the men's gold, churning enormous headline after enormous headline. Who noticed Torvill and Dean moving to fifth in the ice dancing?

Yet here they had to accommodate the knowledge that they'd be seen by a larger audience than they'd known, not just the 12,000 in the rink but an unseen backdrop of millions watching on television. It made them nervous. But by now The Great Lake Placid Disaster had stung The Great

American Public who set themselves to redeem what remained of the good name of The Land of The Brave and Home of the Free. They cheered anything and everything, reserving a special affection for anything and everything British. (A TV programme tried to prove the accommodation in the prison wasn't *that* bad and a British team-member agreed. It's fine, he said, just fine. I caught the programme in an hotel and as he spoke the whole place erupted in approval.)

The Americans responded in full measure to the free dance. Christopher, in striking blue with a natty bow tie, and Jayne in a lighter blue, stirred applause and deserved it. By the end the nerves had long gone. They were enjoying themselves.

They confirmed that in the Worlds at Dortmund a month later — fourth and nearly on the podium. Here, for a wider comparison, are marks set against those of the Dortmund winners, Regoeczy and Sallay.

First compulsory:

Regoeczy, Sallay

5.5   5.5   5.3   5.7   5.3   5.4   5.3   5.4   5.3

Torvill, Dean

5.3   5.4   5.4   5.4   5.5   5.4   5.3   5.2   5.1

Free, artistic impression:

Regoeczy, Sallay

5.9   5.9   5.8   5.9   5.9   5.8   5.8   5.9   5.9

Torvill, Dean

5.7   5.7   5.8   5.5   5.8   5.7   5.7   5.6   5.5

Closer; although that might mean little or much. Certainly, with the propulsion bearing them forward ever more strongly, they might expect to become genuine front-runners after the usual post-Olympics retirements: Regoeczy and Sallay, for instance, and no misunderstanding this time.

Who, though, could foresee where the propulsion would lift Torvill and Dean? He still worked in the police, she still worked for the Norwich Union and as the season ended and the skating fraternity departed the Westfalenhalle, Dortmund, on the week ending 16 March 1980, they had yet to stand on a podium which really counted — European, Olympic or World. Christopher went back on the beat. He could hardly continue to pound it indefinitely.

That summer, with the memories of Gothenburg and Lake Placid and Dortmund already history, Torvill and Dean faced the decision. However

'amateur' Olympic sports pretended to be, you couldn't play at or near the top if you held a full-time job simultaneously. You lacked the time for both and the one distracted from the other. The Soviets neatly circumvented this by calling their sportspeople students, generally of physical culture. The Brits didn't behave like that and while British skaters didn't have to fend totally for themselves they could expect no more than subsistence grants.

Christopher has recorded how he came to dread making arrests because of the subsequent time-consuming paperwork, and, however flexible the police were with time off, however proud of what their PC was achieving, police work remained police work: it was essential to the community and it had to be done properly.

At this point Betty Callaway, through her extensive contacts, secured them a place at Oberstdorf for a few weeks. They'd be at a superb centre housing three rinks, have as much time as they needed on them or work in the gym if they preferred. They'd taste what it might be like as full-time amateurs.

It brought the fundamental decision closer, a decision which would have agonizing consequences. If they ducked it then the very summit of ice dancing would elude them. If they took it they'd run against the ethics of their upbringing: cast away good, secure jobs and — we're in 1980 — the police and the Norwich Union were about as secure as you could get.

To working people of working stock, this might be outrageous or irresponsible or both. Gambling a guaranteed wage and a proper future to sink to subsistence and then stretch that subsistence by going regularly to Oberstdorf could only compound the irresponsibility: casting your future into the clutches of judges prey to who knows what influence, what whims?

Christopher prudently took advice from a Sgt Stone at the station and Sgt Stone — who ought to be remembered, like Janet Sawbridge, for what might not have been — understood, sympathised and comforted. Christopher spent an hour with the Chief Constable outlining the position. He couldn't go on banking days off, holidays, days owing and potential overtime for ever — and even if he did, that wouldn't give him enough time for what he knew had to be done. He felt 'desperate' because he couldn't really afford not to work.

The dilemma: he couldn't afford to work either.

He decided and a deal was done. If he had to leave the police he could do so in three days. Jayne, astonished that he'd really taken the decision, had been working flexi-time at the Norwich Union and sometimes failed even to meet that. She was told she'd have to give a month's notice but,

LEFT AND ABOVE *The free dance was also movement, movement, movement, smoothed, a sort of electrical current running through it* (Colorsport).

taking one thing and another into consideration, could go in three weeks.

Leaving jobs put them both into a strange vacuum, the vacuum of sudden unemployment, although neither would be a burden on society. They never did claim state benefit nor were likely to. *They weren't that kind.* This is not being idealistic or misty eyed. It is just true.

I remember a long telephone conversation with Jayne around this time when, as best I could, I tried to suggest that if push came to shove the *Daily Express*, my newspaper, might be persuaded to use its influence to help; further I remember imploring her not to give up. There was something about Jayne which suggested a formidable future and the same with Christopher. I had not the remotest idea about the extent of that future and, circa 1980, wouldn't have believed it if somebody had told me. But clearly they were good, and getting better, and medals would come. Gold medals? You wouldn't have ventured that — but medals, all right. And Brits don't win many of any colour.

They survived subsistence and in the future, before push really shoved, Nottingham City Council offered them a grant of £8,000 which they could

siphon out up to the Winter Olympics in Sarajevo in 1984 or take as a lump sum. Subsequently they were interviewed by the Council's finance committee and made a pitch for between £13,000 and £14,000. While this was nowhere near enough to sustain them to Sarajevo it was certainly enough to prolong their survival. The Council — and despite reports to the contrary, most councils know the value of £ coins — made an inspired decision of their own. They offered £42,000. That would be enough.

It also provoked a furore and you can easily imagine the grounds. Spendthrifts flinging ratepayers money on flights of fancy for the voluntarily unemployed. A politically biased national newspaper set out to crucify the Council until it discovered some of those fully in favour were in the party of its own bias. (Ice skating judges would understand such moves and counter-moves.) For £42,000 Nottingham City Council gained a publicity coup — up to Sarajevo — worth £42 million or quite possibly £442 million. Putting this more prosaically, the publicity Torvill and Dean brought to Nottingham up to winter 1984 may well have been beyond the Council's entire budget to purchase. Try and buy space on virtually every television channel in the world, much of it at prime time, for many, many days over three years and see how you get on.

It did not soften the risk to Torvill and Dean. If it went wrong they had nothing except a reputation which wouldn't last a season after they'd gone — and, repeating, they'd never been on the big podiums which count. A cameo of a career which ultimately went close and foundered and sank through melting ice. Hands up who remembers how many who've sunk like that? Oberstdorf would be Shangri-la. Torvill and Dean didn't stop being workers. They began. In 1981 the OSP rhythm had been designated the cha-cha-cha and they'd devote three hours a day to that alone. They returned to Britain in the autumn and won the St. Ivel International at Richmond, then a precursor and pointer to the season. Christopher, typically, pronounced himself 'relaxed and confident' as they skated. Their highest marks — 5.9 — were a pointer too.

The British Championships were a formality and they went to Innsbruck in January 1981 for the Europeans. Linichuk and Karponosov hadn't retired, nor had Min and Mo, and the Soviets carried reinforcements for their artillery, Natalia Bestemianova and Andrei Bukin. What slot would they move into? She was slender-legged, shapely and molten, suggestive enough to make you think if she did The Fire Dance the place would catch light, women and children to the exits first, please. He, in the Soviet mould, stood a great deal taller, craggy, a mask and a pillar and an accomplice, all stoops and angles on the ice and off it. He wasn't remote or with-

drawn but we'd need time to understand that.

Innsbruck carried heavy associations. At this rink Curry won gold at the 1976 Winter Olympics and in his way re-defined men's skating, soothing it away from the mechanical towards the balletic. Cousins cemented tenth place that same night and embarked upon his long journey to Lake Placid and the succession. Torvill and Dean would skate here only five years after Curry's re-definition, the memories still fresh. It was a proper setting in a winter city that had twice — 1964 and 1976 — hosted the Olympics. Beyond and above the ornate, pastel-shaded buildings the ski jump loomed from a hillside like an icon remembering what had been.

Victory at Innsbruck over the Soviets. Left Irina Moiseeva and Andrei Minenkov; right Natalia Linichuk with the arm of her partner Gennadi Karponosov round her waist (Colorsport).

What chance had the unemployed, a former copper and a former insurance clerk? We didn't know about their progress at Oberstdorf. When a skating season ends you move to other things, pick it up again in the autumn and miss the bit in the middle, especially if the middle has been happening in Bavaria. We gathered in the neat, cramped cafeteria at the rink (same as Nottingham, formica, tin trays but solid Austrian grub, not a sausage roll or a baked bean on the horizon) and gossiped and projected and doubted.

The consensus: on the balance of probability and assuming nobody else vaulted a few slots, Torvill and Dean would get third or fourth, and either placing would be an achievement under the weight of the three-pronged Soviet assault. (The Brits nicknamed Bestemianova and Bukin *B and B*, but no doubt the connotation escaped the Soviets and they didn't protest.)

Going into the Championship, Christopher said little, masking his feelings. It's what he did, in early 1981. Jayne smiled and seemed uncomfortable to be asked questions. She had not yet grown easy with the demands of celebrity. She'd speak pleasantly enough, revealing absolutely nothing, and drown you in the widest smile. She must have known she seemed vulnerable as a waif, the kind you wanted to cuddle and protect rather than interrogate.

Within a few days such male gallantry had long gone. She was a hell of a sight tougher than the questioners (including me) and never for an instant sacrificed the femininity. It devastated: the sculptured child-girl-woman before you who spoke so politely and with such touching reticence. She seemed hemmed by attention at close quarters and, on the Olympic rink of so many memories, bewitched millions at long range. It takes a bit of coping with, that does.

Not every aspect of Innsbruck suited them — specifically the training rink. This was a temporary 'bubble' attached to the side of the rink proper like a pregnancy. It was cramped, cold and, when the winter sun limped over the Alps around Innsbruck, the bubble dripped. Thawed.

The compulsories were the Westminster Waltz, the Paso Doble and the Rhumba. You might expect the British to capture something as close to home as the Westminster Waltz but there was nothing inevitable about it. The Soviets, hugely able, richly experienced, wonderfully versatile and coming at you in such numbers, had known for a year they'd be skating it and who says nationality gives you the edge, any more than that Americans would always win the Rock 'n' Roll, or Austrians always win the Viennese Waltz? In the event, Torvill and Dean did win it. The marks:

Torvill, Dean

5.7 5.6 5.7 5.4 5.7 5.4 5.4 5.6 5.5

Min and Mo

5.5 5.5 5.6 5.5 5.6 5.5. 5.3 5.5 5.5

Linichuk, Karp

5.4 5.5 5.5 5.4 5.4 5.6 5.4 5.4 5.6

B and B

5.3 5.2 5.3 5.2 5.2 5.3 5.0 5.3 5.3

They'd gone into the Westminster Waltz in the spirit of crusaders, all to gain, and the singular fact that they led the Championships after it disconcerted them because they weren't expecting to. An entirely new pressure arose, that of expectation. They had not experienced this before. Good marks were no longer a bonus. Good marks were the standard, the benchmark.

Their faces tell you everything at Innsbruck (Colorsport).

They skated the Paso Doble 'defensively' and still won it. They were further disconcerted when the British media (about five people) cornered them for an interview which, at this stage of a competition, was unusual. Normally an unstated or heavily stated pact decreed that skaters were left entirely alone during competitions. (This caused problems of its own. In his pomp Cousins had terrible trouble with his version of the compulsory dances, known in men's skating as compulsory figures. Gothenburg, 1980, and for once he got one right. It intoxicated him to such a degree that he vaulted up to where the Press sat and demanded 'how about that then?' We, sworn to the pact, said sorry we couldn't possibly answer questions and then milked this bonus for all it was worth by noting everything he said.)

Now: Innsbruck, 1981, in the fading light of a forgotten day a year on from Gothenburg. Torvill and Dean cornered, eyes darting everywhere, prey almost. 'I feel a little bit more confident because we have an extra year's experience,' Jayne said. 'I feel we have improved all round. I felt more nervous when we'd finished than when we were on the ice.' She might have canvassed much else, but no. One question begged an answer. *What was the difference between you and those Russians?* She touched her hand to her heart and said 'the feeling you have for dance in there'. Not bad for a former insurance clerk who'd been on flexi-time such a short while before.

They feared they'd be slotted downwards by the judges, perhaps because of the impertinence of being in the lead. Wrong. They consolidated during the OSP, no mark of the 18 lower than 5.6 and the average towards 5.7 to 5.8. The free was in no sense an authentic Torvill and Dean masterpiece as we would come to know them but it contained electricity, shimmies which had the audience whooping, gyrations which were frankly provocative, bum-wiggles in the nicest possible taste.

A saxophone wailed. They floated into the slow sequence, undulating to the touch, so close and so personal they made you a voyeur, floated without seeming transition into *Red Sails in the Sunset*, the saxophone wailing on, the undulations closing man to woman until the wail melted into a lowing and you could hear it long after. How judges mark such performances is not for me to say but they had to and they did. Technical merit:

Torvill, Dean

5.8   5.8   5.9   5.9   5.8   5.8   5.8   5.8   5.8

Min and Mo

5.7   5.7   5.8   5.8   5.7   5.7   5.7   5.6   5.8

Artistic impression:

Torvill, Dean

5.8   5.9   5.8   5.9   5.9   5.9   5.9   5.9   5.8

Min and Mo

5.9   5.9   5.9   5.8   5.8   5.9   5.8   5.9   5.9

Judges placings:

Torvill, Dean

1   1   1   1   1   1   1   1   2

Min and Mo

2   2   2   2   3   2   2   1   1

The placing of 2 for Torvill and Dean came from the Soviet judge Igor

Kabanov, and we shall be meeting him again, repeatedly and reluctantly. Judge number five, who scored Min and Mo third, was a Briton, Roy Mason.

On the late evening of 8 February, 1981, Torvill and Dean had gone as near as you can get to eliminating simple, unforced error and within the confines of ice dancing as it was they were good. They *were* European Champions but not outstandingly so: just one more couple who had won it, another on the list, and ice dancing comparatively young.

The first World Championships began as late as 1952 and in those formative years — and beyond — the Brits dominated: Westwood and Demmy, Dewhirst and Slater, Weight and Thomas, Markham and Jones, Towler and Ford. They dominated it until the Soviet Union, pursuing its policy of straddling and pounding most Olympic sports (the prestige factor), turned their attention, their resources and their physical education students to it. No British couple had won the Worlds since 1969, and we are at Innsbruck 12 years later, a long time even on the ice dancing scale, and 'only' the Europeans won. The 1981 Worlds, to be held in Hartford, Connecticut, USA, lay two months distant.

Torvill and Dean had now made their first major impact, via television, on The Great British Public. They were always going to be hard to resist given their unshedable Britishness, their diffidence, their impossible modesty and the spells they could weave; and out-gunning the Soviet artillery added rich undertones and overtones. Whether, prey to the vagaries of judging, ice dancing or any other branch of skating can be truly considered a sport is a moot point, but largely irrelevant when gauging the impact. They leapt off the screen or drew you into the screen and the subsequent modesty *was not resistible* except to people who had made up their minds this thing was candy floss and *you can't convert me to it*. From them, in the fullness of time, Torvill and Dean would make converts, leaving a kernel of implacable agnostics.

I sought them out the day after the European Championships because for the first time the *Daily Express* had caught the impact and wanted to know quite who these people were and the power they wielded. Torvill and Dean sat in a corner of the Holiday Inn, she returned to the child-girl-woman, he loosening up a bit, more comfy with question and answer. One question had to be asked. *What is your relationship?*

Jayne Torvill said exactly these words. 'We're not brother and sister, we're a bit more. It's not a marriage, it's not a boy and his girlfriend. It's not a courting couple. That's not on our schedule.' Whether they had anticipated this question from someone, somewhere and rehearsed the answer

is not clear. What is clear is that the question would come up in interview after interview and each time she mouthed the same words. Some journalists, arriving fresh to it, regarded this as a baring of the soul, a shaft of light, and were dismayed to learn they came to it far down the line: and if you read the words again they reveal something and nothing. It was the way Torvill and Dean wanted it, and the way it was.

Another question would loom interview after interview. *When are you getting married?* Christopher always assumed the responsibility for tackling that and used a distillation of his own, a crisp, no-nonsense non-sequitur. *Not this week.* It alway drew laughter, but like the brother and sister incantation revealed something and nothing.

Ah, but the Holiday Inn, January 1981. A church bell tolls each quarter hour, trams creak by, fur hats bob along the street outside. We sit in a corner and Christopher says he'd taken ribald remarks from other policemen about 'going to have a prance on the ice' but it didn't trouble him. He experienced more 'nightmares' as a policeman than on the ice because people's lives are in play rather than competition slots, podiums and medals. He added that you shouldn't join the police force if you're of a nervous disposition. Jayne quipped impromptu 'yes, and you ran after somebody once and got knocked over, didn't you?' and smiled the consuming smile.

She added that if she was offered a million pounds to go back to being an insurance clerk she'd refuse. I didn't doubt her. Not to mention the publicity on a scale strictly beyond the grasp of Press Relations that was flowing to Nottingham and its City Council. Torvill and Dean were poised to burst budgets.

Around January 1981 she usually took the lead in conversation, handled most of the talking, he listening attentively. To him: *two words are better than four.* You had to extract words from him, play the dentist. *This won't really hurt.* They had already established a telepathy which enabled them to communicate without speaking and this manifested itself in unusual ways. She'd start a sentence, pause and he'd complete it, no modulation or hesitation, only continuity.

Risking a bit, she said 'we quibble more than anything. Sometimes we get a bit hysterical on the ice. I don't shout at Chris. He shouts at me'. Ah, the femininity and also the truth. He could still explode because he would have had to become another man if he didn't. The explosions did not touch the fundamentals or disturb the relationship. She saw the explosions as the way it would be and the fall-out cascaded past her leaving no scars. It is another reason why they could do what they did, and do it with such pre-

cision that my daughter once commented 'it's like watching someone skate with a mirror'.

Articulate Jayne, leading, said of the slow sections 'you can feel the silence. That's when you have the power to carry 10,000 people with you, lift them up and set them down again'. Not bad for a former insurance clerk . . .

And they went to Hartford, Connecticut, went to the 1981 Worlds to refound the British dynasty. Hartford: a 'British' provincial town on another continent, a central cluster of skyscrapers, a snake pit of freeways uncoiling along the belly of the nearby valley, winter sun glinting from a cavalcade of windshields as the morning rush hour mounted. Hartford was homely (homey as Americans say, homely being derogatory) and they plastered stickers everywhere. *Hartford welcomes The World.*

ABOVE LEFT Karen Barber and Nicky Slater, who lived so long in the shadow of Torvill and Dean but never lost their enthusiasm (Supersport).

ABOVE RIGHT Barber and Slater never lost their ability to smile, either, though once Torvill and Dean had gone they'll be cruelly marked down (Supersport).

Linichuk and Karponosov, beaten into third place at Innsbruck, had retired to marry. They were the first couple destroyed by Torvill and Dean. It left Min and Mo, and B and B, without forgetting the entrance of American couple Judy Blumberg and Michael Seibert who were expected to show strongly with the full untrammelled, uncritical, shriek-and-shriek fervour of The Great American Public behind them.

Christopher indulged in a cryptic comment before the competition. 'Innsbruck? What happened there? That's past, gone, and we haven't thought about it since.' Historically the winners of the Europeans are hard to dislodge at the Worlds because the slots tend to carry over even though the judges change. Of the nine at Innsbruck — Swiss, French, Czech, West German, British, Italian, Austrian, Hungarian and Soviet — only Kabanov judged Hartford as well. At Hartford the judges came from West Germany, the United States, Hungary, France, Britain, Canada, Italy, Czechoslovakia and the Soviet Union.

Torvill and Dean struck early and, as it proved, decisively, dominating the first compulsory, the Paso Doble:

Torvill, Dean

5.7   5.8   5.8   5.8   5.6   5.5   5.7   5.7   5.8

Min and Mo

5.6   5.5   5.6   5.8   5.3   5.6   5.6   5.5   5.7

That sixth mark of 5.5, awarded by the Canadian judge, would be the lowest they'd receive in the whole competition and if you're averaging 5.7 to 5.8 sprinkled with 5.9s you'll be extremely difficult to overtake. They led after the compulsories, said they'd enjoyed themselves and felt that the improvement between 1980 and now could be explained by their giving up their jobs. 'We've been training five hours a day,' Jayne added. 'That's the difference.' The 5.9s began in the OSP, their striking rate a good 0.2 of a mark above Min and Mo, upon whom great weight descended. Soviet couples had won every World Championship since 1970 except Dortmund, 1980.

Before the free dance I glimpsed Moiseeva doing press-ups and stretch exercises using the fender of a truck in a hall near the rink. I wished her good luck and she smiled bleakly. She knew her fate, no matter that they'd skate after Torvill and Dean, bestowing an advantage: judges like to keep some leeway so that however magnificent Torvill and Dean might be, Min and Mo would at least have the leeway to aim at. If you have a final group of four couples you can't know who is best until you've seen them all.

That was certainly the theory in 1981. In time Torvill and Dean would destroy even this and render judging a nightmare. But not yet.

Wearing purple — which, like everything else they wore, seemed to suit them — they demonstrated that they'd reached the point where they had it and could flaunt it, although not in any vulgar way because they were incapable of vulgarity. No, it was more of a shedding of inhibitions, their feet movements solving the contradiction of being staccato and smooth at the same time, their body and arm gestures a controlled sequence of flicks and flourishes which had the crowd beating out applause.

Technical merit:

5.8   5.8   5.9   5.9   5.9   5.8   5.8   5.9   5.8

Artistic impression:

5.8   5.8   5.9   5.9   5.8   5.9   5.9   5.8   5.9

Not much leeway for Min and Mo who had to think in terms of 6.0s, and that in an era when they were awarded meagrely and rarely. No skaters — men's, women's, pairs and ice dance — had received one at Innsbruck.

When Torvill and Dean had skated they waited in the dressing rooms, listening to the applause for Min and Mo, hearing what someone has described as a 'gasp' — Blumberg and Seibert fell — then listening to the applause for B and B. Neither Jayne nor Christopher can recall who told them they'd become World Champions but it was probably Betty Callaway. At some point she did come in and said, entirely in character, 'well, we did it'.

Mrs Callaway is not a woman to indulge in flights of fancy. Asked about the future she hauled everything back down to terra firma. 'We shall have to work harder.'

Hartford was an end as well as a beginning. Torvill and Dean's free programme existed entirely within the constrictions, four distinct changes of tempo. It began with jazz from *Fame*, hard and sharp and urgent, slowed to the wail of *Caravan*, glided into *Red Sails in the Sunset* and romped through *Swing, Swing, Swing* to the big finish. It was an unremarkable programme in that sense, and similar in tone and scope to the programmes the others were doing. Torvill and Dean simply did theirs better.

Who could guess, as the fraternity dispersed from Hartford, Connecticut, that something restless would stir inside the former policeman and very soon he'd expand the constrictions and then virtually destroy them? Or that within six months he and Jayne would have enough propulsion to carry a global audience, lift them up and set them down again at

LEFT A last look at the way they were, classically within the confines of ice dancing. Within a year they'd have changed all that – convulsively (Colorsport).

will? Or that the propulsion would be harnessed into artistry of a kind never imagined, leaving all the opposition — Soviet, American, Canadian, French, didn't matter from where — breathless in their wake, never to catch up?

Torvill and Dean wouldn't be a step ahead, they'd constantly be a dimension ahead.

It was no way to think as the hire cars and limos took the fraternity down Interstate 91, past comfortingly familiar names for Brits — Glastonbury, Wallingford, Bridgeport — to JFK Airport and the flight home. Another season, just another new winning couple in the succession from 1952.

Wrong.

3

Haunting the World

RICHMOND ICE RINK, LIKE THE STADIUM AT NOTTINGHAM, was a sombre edifice and normally no place for espionage. The Thames flowed silently beside it and, over a broad stone bridge, the semi-chic semi-suburban contours of Richmond nestled, spread up a long incline. Tall old houses fringed the Thames and the rink, facing them across it, had the air of a dignified widow. To one end of this rink a window showed stained glass figures of skaters in various poses, fashionable of an era but now, autumn 1981, fussily ornate and very dated.

The surround to the ice surface was narrow, a little walkway and a few rows of seats to each side; and above, on another tier, a pre-war sort of balcony. On it Betty Callaway spied a Soviet camera crew preparing to film Torvill and Dean doing their new Original Set Pattern. She realised immediately that the film would be transmitted to Moscow for careful dissection — enormous value to Min and Mo and B and B in the European Championships at Lyons and the World Championships at Copenhagen.

She knew that film of Torvill and Dean's compulsory dances offered only academic interest since everybody had to skate them and they remained so technical that you wouldn't — couldn't — allow other couples to influence you. She knew equally that the free dance was so personal that you couldn't copy it, but the OSP, this year the blues, might give the Soviets clue after clue about how the blues really should be handled.

Mrs Callaway betook herself to the balcony where she found a burly man and a burly woman. She had no authority to order them to stop filming. It's a free country. She positioned herself as near to their camera as she could and *glowered*. Mrs Callaway has an acerbic, chilly, schoolma'mish glower when she wants. The Soviets retreated in some confusion, not to be seen again.

The Callaway confrontation occurred at the St.Ivel International which, as we've seen, represented the first serious competition of a season and revealed what

RIGHT The unveiling of the new era, the Torvill and Dean era. They launch Mack and Mabel *at the St. Ivel competition, Richmond, as a prelude to the 1982 season (Don Morley).*

couples had prepared during the summer. During the St.Ivel, Richmond had two strands woven into it: curiosity and anticipation. Here, too, Torvill and Dean would unveil their free programme which, one naturally assumed, would obey the classical dictum, four pieces of music with differing tempos.

Secrecy surrounds much of ice skating and while a free dance can't be stolen and used by others — nobody would dare do that — you don't show your hand until you have to. Nor is the music for this year's free dance necessarily something you've found this year. You might have heard a piece long ago and thought *that's nice* or *that's interesting* or *maybe we can use that one day*. You don't tell outsiders but you do remember.

In fact, some two years before, hunting around Radio Nottingham's sound library for music, they'd come upon *Mack and Mabel*, a Broadway musical by Jerry Herman of dubious provenance. It ran nine days and folded. The story recaptured the tempestuous affair between Mack Sennett of silent picture fame and Mabel Normand, his leading lady. Torvill and Dean liked the music and saw the possibilities but felt they weren't ready to use it.

With the Hartford World Championships safely behind them, they considered *Mack and Mabel* again and, better, Christopher had a tape of it. They could have that played during training sessions, allowing them to experiment, see where they might take it. The music grew on them, particularly one part where 'just fooling around'

Mack and Mabel portrayed many moods but it broke the confines because it was one continuous piece. 'We'd known the music for about three years and it seemed right to do it,' Dean said (Don Morley).

66

they invented a sequence: he leant forward, she angled herself until she lay onto his back and she did the scissors four times, they rose, she moved to the other side and they repeated it, her feet tap-tap-tapping. Spectators in all the corners of the earth would adore the sheer cheekiness.

Christopher pondered *Mack and Mabel*, pondered it again and made a decision as fundamental as leaving the police force. They'd use only *Mack and Mabel*. At first Betty Callaway and Jayne nursed profound misgivings, their instincts preferring a more conservative course — at a minimum working a Rhumba into it somewhere. Christopher pondered and persisted, they desisted and ice dancing changed at that moment.

An urgent question had to be answered. Was it legal? If it wasn't, the Soviets would seize on that and very likely protest it into oblivion or the judges would punish the illegality in their marks. Torvill and Dean approached two experienced British judges who lived not far from Nottingham and asked if they'd come along and pass a verdict. Torvill and Dean received immediate reassurance, not only that it was within the rules but a glory to behold.

At the St.Ivel, they skated Larry Adler's recording of *Summertime Blues* — the mouth-organ yearning — at the slowest pace permitted, giving it a languid sensuousness which conjured a 6.0. *Mack and Mabel*, a storm of a free programme, conjured three 6.0s and these from Soviet, Canadian and Austrian judges. That was of two-fold importance. Now international judges accepted its legality and, because they were international, this was no Brits hyping Brits for the battles ahead, flinging maximums into the air to frighten the opposition. In fact *Mack and Mabel* was such a storm that Jayne 'got completely carried away. I was enjoying myself so much I didn't realise we were near the end of it!'

The British Championships at Nottingham, six weeks after the St.Ivel, were a formality again although only six couples competed. The organisers condensed the three sections into a single evening, making the Championships an endurance test. Christopher gathered what remained of his strength for the free and it became a triumph, two 6.0s for technical merit and a thunderous seven 6.0s for artistic impression.

In four minutes they removed any limitations to the rest of their careers and perhaps their lives.

A week later they attempted something audacious by trying to become the first dancers to win (or attempt to win) a Gold Star, a hallowed award of absolute excellence which only a handful of solo skaters had ever tried. Why do this? 'To keep them on their toes,' Callaway insisted, not to mention that success would increase their reputations commensurately.

To achieve it Torvill and Dean must skate the three compulsory dances from the previous season, the three from the current season and the OSP and the free — all in 40 minutes. Nor did it end there. They must receive no mark lower than 5.2 for the compulsories and none lower than 5.5 for the free. You don't have to belabour this to understand its inherent difficulties. Nottingham Stadium would be a compression chamber.

That Sunday afternoon in late November some 1,000 spectators came to watch this strange, compelling and slightly surreal ritual. Five judges sat impassive, noting their marks *but not showing them*. Torvill and Dean had no idea how they were doing. At the end a little flurry of activity rose among the judges. Were they summoning courage to say *no, sorry, you failed*? What were they discussing? The judges called Torvill and Dean over and invited them to re-skate one compulsory — the music hadn't been properly co-ordinated between two loudspeakers. You don't have to belabour this to understand its sting, just when you thought it was all over.

They might have heard an echo of Janet Sawbridge and the Inter-gold so

ABOVE LEFT European crowds surrendered en masse to Mack and Mabel, *to its richness of gestures as well as its excitement* (Wilfried Witters).

ABOVE RIGHT Here is the excitement (Wilfried Witters).

long ago which nearly went so wrong, the echo saying *summon yourself, do it, do it*.

That Sunday afternoon they did it again, just like that. As someone has said, great performers are the ones who can give great performances all the time, not just when their chemistry works or the moon's in the right conjunction. The result produced a cheer louder than you'd think 1,000 could muster. The Gold Star had been properly conquered.

In their usual economy of words they said 'well, that was hard work'.

Lyons in January 1982: a southern city, a hint of Spring in the air already and, the French being French, for the European Championships they decided to outdo the hospitality ever known at any sporting event by persuading a tidal wave of Beaujolais growers to come down the autoroute daily with their wares for sampling, and please have another bottle or two. This may explain why some of the reporting lacked objectivity and it may not. Cold sober, you found it increasingly difficult to be objective about Torvill and Dean, and the closer you were the more the difficulty. It was a compound of affection, admiration and awe.

Again they struck early and decisively, winning the first compulsory, the blues (interestingly in 1982 the tempo for the OSP, too, as we've seen). They reached such ease during this compulsory that Callaway, attentive at the rinkside and monitoring every nuance, could not hear their blades even whispering over the ice. By the second dance, the Yankee Polka, the marks homed in on 5.8 with two plump 5.9s.

During the warm-up for the OSP — couples are drawn to skate in groups, normally of four or five, and there's a warm-up between each group — they startled everyone by preparing separately, he motoring off in one direction, she in another. Normally couples warmed-up together, going through segments of their programme. Since Torvill and Dean prepared themselves before training by skating separately, they reasoned why not in competitions? Another echo: *Be strong enough to be yourself, approach it in the way suiting you*.

They startled the crowd much more profoundly when they did skate, Jayne feeling in a 'trance,' Christopher feeling in a 'dream'. They woke to see three 6.0s for presentation. The crowd, prey to Gallic outbursts of emotion, burst, their noise flooding the entire rink and going up and up a scale until, momentarily, it seemed genuine hysteria would claim them. As I say, objectivity was a hard task — for spectators, fellow skaters, judges, officials, the whole media, and maybe Torvill and Dean themselves. And we hadn't had the free, the storm and the big finish yet. The BBC prepared to put the Nine O'Clock News back to transmit it live . . .

Images of *Mack and Mabel* that night: Torvill and Dean flow together and might be going to kiss, let the music pluck the kiss away before lips can touch; let the music urgently transport them into the whirl and twirl of dervishes, his hair lapping onto his forehead, her hair bob-bounce-bobbing; he lifts and turns her in a single, fluid, unbroken movement, they rotate, all four arms out-stretched in front of them, flow into a neat step-sequence, she in front, he behind, left-legs forward in unison then right-legs, left-right-left-right: turn at the end of the rink, kick the air, whirl and twirl again, skim into the back-to-back scissors, tap-tap-tap, the crowd bellowing them on, *adoring* the cheekiness. Technical merit:

5.9   5.9   5.9   6.0   6.0   5.9   6.0   5.9   5.9

They sat where tradition demanded they sat, in the specially created alcove decorated by the fronds of shrubs — which skaters who've just finished go to. They sat on a plain seat facing the scoreboard and facing a television camera placed to catch their expressions, illuminate

ABOVE LEFT The compulsory dances during the British Championships at Nottingham in autumn 1982 — prelude to the great assault of 1983. Betty Callaway watches, lost in thought (Colorsport).

ABOVE RIGHT By now they had mastered the technical intricacies of the compulsories to an astonishing degree and carried them off with a smile (Colorsport).

each bead of sweat, each tear-drop or smile or hug: human reaction in cinemascope. They wore anoraks slung loosely over their shoulders and waited for the artistic impression. The marks, white quartz figures, sprang up like machine-gun fire and reverberated like machine-gun fire, too.

6.0   6.0   6.0   6.0   6.0   5.9   6.0   6.0   6.0

Jayne's face peeled into a valley of a smile, relief and incredulity mixed. Callaway leant across in an almost involuntary jerking movement of reflex, Christopher bent and kissed Jayne on the cheek. Torvill and Dean had ascended to an unexplored plateau. Their total of fourteen 6.0s in the Championships sent historians scurrying and burrowing for precedents and none could be found. The French had surrendered to them en masse, been lifted up and then set down again — and without doubt the more restrained, understated Danes would do the same at Copenhagen. On a more pragmatic level, who do you think was the judge who didn't hoist a 6.0 for artistic impression? Our old 'friend' Igor Kabanov.

They could conjure anything they wanted, seeming to be completely boneless if that was what they felt was required (Wilfried Witters).

It is time, high time, to interrupt the flow of the narrative again and examine those nine expressionless people arranged in a row — the judges. Their part is by definition crucial and yet surrounded by a degree of mystery, not to mention dark and sinister political motives of which they've constantly been suspected.

Superficially judging is obvious enough. A country is awarded a judge for an international competition on the strength of where that country's skaters finished in the competition the year before, and they mark on a scale up to 6.0.

Judging is subjective, and therefore if bias exists it can never be finitely proved. Every judge has the perfect defence. *I marked what I saw.* What you can prove by scrutinising the marks is whether a judge is out of step with the other eight and whether the judge constantly favours his or her own nationals. The International Skating Union did just this in the late 1970s and banned Soviet judges for a year.

There's a folklore, also incapable of proof that, certainly until Communism melted in Eastern Europe, judges tended to vote according to the Cold War bloc they came from. So a Czech or Hungarian or Polish judge would look favourably upon the skaters of Mother Russia; and a West German, Swiss or Canadian judge might look just as favourably westwards.

Like a game of unknowns, you'd hear people calculating how many judges they had and how many we had. Did it really work like that? We simply don't know. Nor did it end there. If a judge did want to favour their national it could be done more subtly than flaying the opposition in an obvious way. You could play all manner of permutations within the marking, each judge giving — to select Hartford, 1981 at random — a total of 147 marks during the whole competition.

From time to time the idea was floated that the highest and lowest marks from each set of nine should be discarded, making bias more difficult, but whatever the machinations a curiosity arose. By general consent the right winners invariably emerged in ice dancing, however they were arrived at, and rarely did disputes exist about the order of the first three. Further down, deep into the jostling for slots you'd wonder, however.

Using Hartford again, these are the marks of the British and Soviet (Kabanov, course) judges for their respective nationals:

	Torvill and Dean		Moiseeva and Minenkov	
	Brit	Sov	Brit	Sov
First compulsory	5.6	5.7	5.3	5.5
Second compulsory	5.7	5.7	5.6	5.7
Third compulsory	5.8	5.7	5.7	5.7
OSP, composition	5.9	5.7	5.7	5.8
OSP, presentation	5.8	5.7	5.8	5.8
Free, technical	5.9	5.9	5.7	5.9
Free, artistic	5.8	5.8	5.7	5.9

ABOVE LEFT But Christopher had backbone in both senses of the word, strong backbone (Colorsport).

ABOVE RIGHT By 1983 it was clear they had become genuine artists in the big sense (Colorsport).

At no stage did the British judge place Min and Mo higher than Torvill and Dean, but the Soviet judge did three times (compare Kabanov's two columns and how he saw the OSP composition, the OSP presentation and the artistic free). I must repeat: you can wring many meanings out of dried statistics and in no sense am I casting doubts on the integrity of these two judges. The fact remained, however, that because of the subjective nature of the thing *a judge couldn't prove his own honesty any more than others could prove bias.*

It seems a reasonable assumption, however, that if a western country's skating association attempted to place overt external pressure on 'their' judge they took a great risk. They might be told to go to hell or chance exposure; and anyway we didn't behave like that.

No such niceties obtained on the other side of the Iron Curtain, as we now know from athletics (where sportspeople had little choice in their chosen activity, and as it would seem, no choice in whether they took banned substances). Consider now the position of the Eastern Bloc judge, a product, surely, of the same general mentality. He or she was granted precious permission to travel, stay in the best hotels, sup at the best watering holes, enjoy a measure of fame and perhaps pick up expenses in hard currency. Cumulatively it amounted to something you'd be reluctant to sacrifice, the more so since all your association had to do was pick another judge to

replace you next year, bestowing all the privileges on them as they were withdrawn from you.

I've explored this for another reason, too. Between Lyons in 1982 and Torvill and Dean's last competitive appearance of their 'first' ice dancing career — Ottawa and the Worlds in March 1984 — each championship would be a British-Soviet struggle or a British-Soviet-American struggle.

Just to complicate this (though briefly) a new system was employed at Copenhagen, the number of judges cut to seven — or rather two batches of seven, the first taking the compulsories and OSP, the second the free dance. Only one judge, the Swiss, sat in both batches. The Soviets had no judge in the first, Kabanov in the second. (The experiment of having only seven judges wouldn't be repeated; in future it moved back to the traditional nine.)

After Lyons, Betty Callaway erected a protective wall. Torvill and Dean returned to Oberstdorf to train and she wouldn't even tell them when they'd been on television at home, something happening a lot. The wall kept distractions and intruders at bay as Callaway kept her eye on the main purpose: train, improve, win.

By the 1982 Worlds at Copenhagen, Torvill and Dean had, without ever courting it, dug so much interest that it threatened to engulf them. They were photogenic, good looking and they won gold medals: everything all at once. The BBC, who'd covered ice skating for decades as part of their regular service, were joined by ITV — the stimulation of interest as intense as that. A competition within a competition arose. Who could get more of Torvill and Dean, who could persuade them to pose by the Mermaid, who could get them shopping? Who could get the best interview?

Because of what Torvill and Dean were, everyone could feed off the feast — radio, women's magazines, sports magazines, gossip diaries, television documentaries, daily papers, Sunday papers, Nottingham's local papers, newshounds, sports hounds and feature writers. Copenhagen airport would be a busy place, bristling with unfamiliar faces. Before Copenhagen *Woman* magazine interviewed them (the issue fortuitously also containing an article on Winter Salad Surprises) and got the brother and sister incantation . . .

It left in suspended animation the questions which more and more people clamoured to have answered and which were posed more and more insistently. Had they been in love? Were they still in love? Were they not in love? Were they to become engaged? And, the big finish, would they marry? 'Not this week', every time.

Perhaps they sensed that people wanted them to be in love, wanted, in a grim world driven by daily disasters, a fairy tale which came true. Torvill

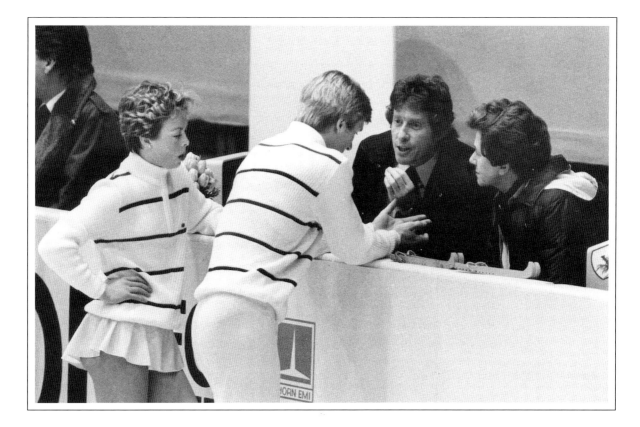

The team discuss Barnum, *the circus which brought the big top to the rink. Michael Crawford (technical adviser!) makes a point while Betty Callaway listens intently (Colorsport).*

and Dean couldn't help with that, only move lock-step into the incantation.

To get close to them, be accepted and trusted, you needed to gain admission to what Betty Callaway termed the 'family'. It comprised people who'd been around for a while and whose motivation was the skating. The media invasion would bring cold waters with sharks in it looking for a quick headline, a revelation, whatever the sharks could get their teeth into. (One pair of sharks scoured Nottingham seeking sexual revelations, for instance, and the best they could do was suggest Torvill and Dean had once been caught in the back of a car. Nice, eh?)

If you were 'family' Torvill and Dean would be entirely relaxed with you, pleased to see you, share a pot of coffee, discuss this and that without tension. They knew that on the record was on the record but off the record wouldn't be appearing anywhere, anytime. To the strangers and occasional sharks who came, they gave a wonderful verbal performance, answering skating questions in their own perceptive way and deflecting personal questions with short, sharp phrases which were also cul-de-sacs, especially

savouring *brother and sister* and *not this week*. They knew it worked, and it did, from Copenhagen to Ottawa and all places in between.

The 'family' was a tight-knit thing, separating insiders and outsiders, and no tighter than at its core: Torvill and Dean themselves. Once he described their relationship as 'platonic', but added 'we don't let outsiders get emotionally involved with us because it wouldn't work. If you take your emotions somewhere else you're taking away from what you've got together'.

Such sentiments only fuelled the clamour to *really* know. How could a handsome couple spend up to five hours a day touching each other — as in training they were obliged to do — and not be involved? How could they spend days and weeks isolated in Bavaria and not be involved? How could they be so close, mentally and physically, to communicate through a kind of telepathy and not be involved? How could they act as lovers so profoundly

BELOW LEFT Barnum *was the most spectacular thing they'd created so far, defying gravity* (Colorsport).

BELOW RIGHT Some of the movements were so complicated you needed still photographs to appreciate them in full. See for yourself (Colorsport).

Torvill and Dean missed the 1983 Europeans at Dortmund – she injured her shoulder – and that only spiced Helsinki. Everyone wanted to know what they'd do. Here they are preparing (Supersport).

on the ice and not be lovers off it? How was that possible?

Fuelling it further, Christopher was a real man, which ice dancers tend to be (but, alas, not all singles skaters: John Curry made little secret of his preferences and it cost him his life). Jayne was a real woman, a cocktail of a creature with the merriest laugh you ever saw, a stern countenance when she needed it and a bearing of exquisite personal dignity. I never once heard her saying anything mean or ungracious. (A very sophisticated West German couple trained with them at Oberstdorf, the young woman was gorgeous and, socially, dressed like a Chanel advertisement. She was asked what she'd learnt from Jayne, meaning about improving her skating, but instead she said 'how to behave like a *lady*'.)

So: Copenhagen, a Baltic city still deep into winter this March and its airport disgorging more and more unfamiliar faces. Nor did Torvill and Dean float serenely through.

The British and Americans were drawn to practice together and one American couple resolutely refused to do anything except bomb round regardless of the other couples. This is not as trivial as it sounds. Skates are sharp, ice is as hard as it ever was, and if you're knocked down you risk serious injury. Mrs Callaway sorted that out. If you can stare down a burly Soviet film crew, errant Americans are no problem. That resolved, a second problem arose. In practice Torvill and Dean couldn't hear the beginning of *Mack and Mabel* and their request for a re-skate was denied. Mrs Callaway took that in hand too.

During a warm-up for the compulsory dances

In 1983 the Original Set Pattern was Rock 'n' Roll and Torvill and Dean rocked 'em even though in the Worlds at Helsinki she skated with a strapped shoulder — disguised, of course; and you can't see it, can you? (Colorsport).

Christopher actually fell, and I use the word actually in no devalued sense. At their level, to succumb to an elementary human error like that seemed unthinkable. He passed it off (as he was always going to pass it off) in the economy of words. 'It woke me up and got my adrenalin going.' Callaway, swiftly erecting the protective wall, murmured — down-beat, voice flat — *I don't quite understand what this fuss is about. They fall in training at Oberstdorf more often than you'd think. Do you imagine they never fall?* End of sensational development.

They'd already won the first compulsory, the blues, with four marks at 5.8 and three at 5.9, B and B overhauling Min and Mo for second place but a distance behind: two 5.5s, three 5.6s, a 5.7, a 5.8.

Torvill and Dean approached the Yankee Polka, next, a 'bit more carefully' after the fall and up came a 5.6, a 5.8, the rest 5.9s. The 5.6 was awarded by a Canadian, and there was a nagging feeling that she might have been right, the others seduced by Torvill and Dean's reputation. This Canadian gave B and B 5.5 in the Yankee Polka but Blumberg and Seibert 5.7 — the only mark of the seven judges above Torvill and Dean.

Summertime Blues stunned the rink: the coiling and uncoiling to the mouth-organ, the submerging into the wail and yearn of that mouth-organ; boneless movement spreading hot and lazy days into a cold rink outside a cold city. The crowd followed it in absolute silence, in a trance themselves. They didn't even cough.

When it was done, the fraternity babbled helplessly about masterpieces, about you'd never see the like again, searched for words and ways to quantify this impact and never really did find them. And up they came, five 6.0s for presentation. Consider: in 1980 Regoeczy and Sallay had received no higher than 5.8, in 1981 Torvill and Dean no higher than a single 5.9.

Barring more elementary human errors, the 1982 World Championships had lost all meaning as a contest. It became a festival and a celebration as *Mack and Mabel* convulsed the rink, no silence now but applause and laughter (at the scissors), and up they came, seven 5.9s for technical merit (out of seven, remember), five 6.0s for artistic impression (Kabanov would go no higher than 5.9 and neither would the West German). They were still on the ice gathering bouquets of flowers proffered by spectators who'd rushed to rinkside. He turned and waved and she continued towards the next bouquet.

Afterwards, producing one of those throw-away lines which were so typical of them and which left listeners speechless, Jayne said 'we hope we can improve. It's nice to have a new programme to look forward to for 1983'.

Nobody, they included, knew what that would be.

They set off on the traditional International Skating Union champions' tour almost immediately after Copenhagen. It lasted three weeks, covered large tracts of Europe and began in Moscow, where Torvill and Dean took the opportunity to watch the State Circus. As they sat enjoying it Christopher mused *circus, circus, that's interesting, that's an interesting theme.*

During the tour he acquired a tape of the popular musical *Barnum*, then playing at the London Palladium with Michael Crawford in the leading role. The fact that the tape was French, and thus had French vocals on it, mattered nothing because he was only interested in the music. The tour over, Torvill and Dean decided to make a positive move. They'd go and watch *Barnum* at the Palladium.

ABOVE LEFT They also practised their exhibition routine (Supersport).

ABOVE RIGHT Barnum *had the crowd clapping at Helsinki instants after it started — and the crowd never stopped* (Supersport).

Chance and improbability pursued them. During the interval, as is the wont of many stage people, Crawford peeked out from the curtain to see who was in tonight and recognised them from *Mack and Mabel*, which he admired. He sent word that if they'd like to join him after the show he'd like to meet them.

They went.

Torvill and Dean are very easy to get on with, Crawford doesn't give himself the airs and graces of superstardom and within a few minutes they'd known each other for years. They shared much. Each were performers with audiences to satisfy, each looking for that elusive, maddening, intransient thing they each called perfection. Crawford was embraced into the 'family' and, when they told him they'd come because they were thinking of using the *Barnum* music, an offer of his help gushed out of him.

The importance of this help cannot be under-estimated, as we shall see.

A moment of ego-breaking had, however, to be overcome. They explained that they needed only the music, not a recording of Crawford singing it, because no vocals are allowed: and if you can picture Crawford's face, I'm sure you can picture it creasing into a smile at that. Whatever, he took it in good part and later rang and said *why don't you come down to the Palladium and have another look?*

They went, this time with Betty Callaway, but in conversation afterwards discovered what might have been a terminal problem. No tapes existed of the music alone. Crawford, bubbling with enthusiasm, suggested that Michael Reed, *Barnum*'s musical director, might be willing to put together some

Barnum *was cheeky, impish, experimental* (Colorsport).

musicians, secure a studio and record it specially. Reed would write the music and score it. Reed arrived and, bubbling too, said he'd be delighted, would be happy to work without charge but couldn't ask the musicians to do the same. The musicians would cost £1,000.

Torvill and Dean returned to Oberstdorf and awaited the date of the recording — in London. One of them would have to be there. Christopher made a provocative policy decision. Jayne would go to the session alone and (wink, nudge) bear the full responsibility for the quality of what she brought back. He reasoned that she was more demanding about music than he. His view, ordinarily: the music's OK. If he went to London and the quality wasn't to her liking he'd spend the whole winter with her reminding him of it.

He drove her to Munich where she took the flight to Heathrow. At Heathrow, walking towards customs, she instinctively looked over her shoulder for him. He wasn't there. It struck her then, struck her forcibly. *It was the first time for four years they had been apart.* That endures as something astonishing. How many married couples can say the same?

She and Callaway journeyed to the recording studio where Crawford joined them and Reed set to work. He knew his business and knew how the pieces — recorded separately — would sound when put together the following day. Jayne moved through an array of sensations: having a mini-orchestra at her bidding, with Reed enquiring *do you like this like this or do you like it like that?* The finished product sounded loaded and larded with promise. She gave a copy to Crawford and he expressed delight, something reassuring.

She flew back to Munich where Christopher waited. They pushed the cassette into the car stereo and now they both felt the promise as *Barnum* echoed on the drive to Oberstdorf.

Day after day they began to create the programme to it but they needed Crawford. To keep the programme a secret they went to Peterborough — a quiet, discreet, out-of-the-way rink — where Crawford could join them. He donned plimsolls and tiptoed onto the ice to demonstrate how to mime putting on clowns' make-up, walk the tightrope, juggle. He used his arms and body, employed graphic gesturing and they saw how it was done. 'Jayne is a brave girl,' he'd say, 'but we had to cut out a couple of things because they were too dangerous.' However one spectacular move where her head descended to within inches of the ice stayed in although Crawford thought that, too, was dangerous.

They didn't unveil *Barnum* at the St. Ivel, where they skated *Mack and Mabel* as an exhibition instead and passed word to journalists considered to

ABOVE LEFT **Barnum** *was massive but disciplined movement, a demonstration of the possibilities of balance* (Colorsport).

ABOVE RIGHT Sneak preview. After Helsinki they'd go away and produce something which produced this (Supersport).

be in the 'family' that they should be at Nottingham the day before the British Championships, or rather at the pub opposite the Stadium.

This chat enabled Torvill and Dean to break the secret and announce *we're doing Barnum*. It gave them the chance to offer their thanks publicly to Crawford and Reed and also explain why and how they'd selected it, the moves and counter-moves, the problems and solutions from the Moscow Circus all the way to here.

Copenhagen had fuelled the interest in them to an entirely new pitch. There was — now — an unquestioned need to make a formal announcement of the free dance to slake the thirst of thousands, no doubt millions, in Britain who wanted to know what it was and why it was. The fact that Crawford, a television celebrity familiar in every home as well as star of *Barnum*, had been an active participant spiced this richly. Torvill and Dean and Crawford would have to be an amazing treble-act.

It was.

They also discussed the OSP, for which, in an open challenge to see what skaters could really do, the International Skating Union had picked Rock 'n' Roll. The mood Torvill and Dean were in, it might have been chosen just for them. They'd glory in what they made of it, real rockers, conjuring the 1950s as if the 1950s had never gone away. Yes, they'd show what they could really do.

Before the competition Crawford sent a telegram. *I'm with you every step of the way*.

They dominated the compulsories and made the Stadium into a rock concert in the OSP, a special achievement because of their self-imposed physical demands: three and a half minutes of frenetic movement testing their stamina and, being Rock 'n' Roll, no slow section to get their breath back. When they'd put the music together they couldn't find a place to cut it without unbalancing the overall effect so they went the three and a half minutes instead. Up came two 6.0s for presentation.

The free dance went well enough by earthly standards but not to their satisfaction. Jayne even made a slip. At the instant she should have been leaning over his back she

Callaway and Crawford — caught a moment or two after victory at Helsinki, Crawford with the biggest smile in the world and getting bigger by the moment (Supersport).

slithered. Maybe that set the tone. She worried, too, that her costume wouldn't survive the stretching *Barnum* demanded and found herself thinking about that as she skated.

The full glory of Barnum *revealed when they skated it as an exhibition at Richmond (Supersport).*

Picture it, however: the Stadium absolutely full, the ranks of seats near the ice pressing an intimate atmosphere onto the skaters, a Nottingham crowd paying their homage to their own kind, the former copper and the former insurance clerk from just up the road. Jayne's slip precluded an array of 6.0s but they did get one, the rest 5.9.

What would they do in the 1983 Europeans at Dortmund? An unanswered question — it was the one they missed. In training at Oberstdorf they got a difficult lift wrong and she hammered onto the ice, visibly hurt. Christopher scooped her up and ferried her off and a few moments later the pain made her cry. Nobody understood better than he Jayne's fibre, her physical (and mental) toughness. When he saw the tears the seriousness struck him as hard as she'd struck the ice. She'd damaged her leg and shoulder but escaped without broken bones.

She mended quickly, as fit sportspeople tend to do, but when they

returned to ice she fell once more, not so badly but another fall. It disturbed their confidence in re-rehearsing the lift and her arm began to hurt again.

Dortmund melted.

They stayed in Oberstdorf and chose not to watch the Europeans on television. Whatever the others did in the Westfalenhalle wouldn't clutter or influence their thinking, wouldn't subconsciously insinuate this impression or that. *Be strong enough to be yourself.* B and B won.

The Worlds in Helsinki — so cold that enough ice lay outside to have held the Championships at any cross-roads — beckoned with a special anticipation. In the cyclical season the slots have been pretty well assigned through the national championships and the Europeans, and while these slots are never absolute the front runners tend to stay front-runners, the middle of the pack jostles, the lowly might hope to rise a slot or two. In sum, minimal movement. Before the Worlds, a knowing member of the fraternity will give you the top 10 and not be far wrong. Torvill and Dean had their formidable reputation, the expected victory in the British Championships (carrying no credence beyond that, front-runners are expected to win domestically) but no slot from the Europeans; and no continental judge had passed judgement on their Rock 'n' Roll or *Barnum*.

The rink was modern and cavernous. A big stage suited Torvill and Dean just as it suited *Barnum* itself. The bigger the area the greater the impact.

A year on from Copenhagen, Helsinki airport bristled with faces familiar and unfamiliar, the feast about to be laid out again, more fodder this time than Copenhagen because during the 12 months between, Torvill and Dean had grown further, not forgetting Michael Crawford and the spicing his presence brought.

When Torvill and Dean arrived they confessed they'd avoided seeing film of Dortmund, never mind the television coverage. They didn't say (they wouldn't) that they avoided the people they knew (and people they didn't know) because all those people would ask about Jayne's shoulder and repeating an incantation about the shoulder's condition would be a wasteful distraction, not forgetting that the shoulder wasn't as well as it might have been (but you'd have had to pull their teeth to extract that). They did say that the dreaded movement which caused the falls had been exorcised.

Crawford arrived and wished to deflect no attention from them — a paradox, them avoiding attention as best they could. He booked into the official hotel, went to his room and stayed there. Soon enough he realised (as he

RIGHT *A last look at* Barnum *and Torvill and Dean's gestures seem to say everything: s'wonderful, s'marvellous* (Supersport).

ABOVE LEFT A look ahead to the Olympic Year, 1984. They'll skate Bolero *and here practise it before the European Championships in Budapest* (Supersport).

ABOVE RIGHT Bolero *captivated Budapest and left them howling for more. Alas, in competitions you can't skate encores* (Supersport).

would) that he couldn't escape questioning and so, tactically, decided it was better to get it over with. He gave an impromptu little talk charting his part — modesty entirely comparable with that of Torvill and Dean — and, a warming touch, amused us by revealing that he referred to Betty Callaway as Harry.

Pardon? Harry? Yes, no mistake. An invented name because Crawford had been in a much-loved television comedy *Some Mothers Do 'av' em* where he played the hapless and accident-prone husband of a wife called Betty. This stayed with him so vividly that saying Betty made him dissolve. A measure of Crawford: consummate performer, controller of the parts he played, demonstrator of mime, but he couldn't completely shed his own creations and was honest enough to admit it.

The compulsories were properly triumphal. Christopher set himself the personal goal of he and Jayne forcing a 6.0, never done before in a compulsory (see the previous chapter, Linichuk and Karponosov, Zagreb, 1979, to appreciate how far we've come). They might have done it in the Argentine tango but skated early and couldn't escape the judges' leeway.

Jayne wore a discreet shoulder-strap, designed to prevent anyone see-

ing it, for the OSP. Picture three and a half minutes of relentless Rock 'n' Roll with that. They plundered the OSP, surviving along the way an instant of anxiety when he reached for her and feared he might tear her skirt. The crowd pounded out the beat and their pounding filled the cavernous rink, sonic booms, the big noise bouncing back at you off the walls. And up they came, a clutch of 5.9s and a 6.0 for composition. What would nine judges do with the presentation? We knew in a trice. They bowed to it.

6.0   6.0   6.0   6.0   6.0   5.9   5.9   6.0   5.9

This, again, had not been seen before and, until then, had been conjectural rather than attainable. Comparison, Regoeczy and Sallay, 1980:

5.6   5.8   5.7   5.8   5.6   5.7   5.7   5.7   5.7

Christopher retreated onto (or didn't rise above) terra firma afterwards, piling ice blocks onto any external fervour. 'It went OK. There is never anything to say when it goes right.' Under harder questioning he conceded the crowd's reaction had been 'pleasing'.

You might be forming the wrong impression. Neither Torvill nor Dean were monosyllabic. They weren't footballers grappling with the complexities of speaking simple sentences, but they erected their own protective wall behind the wall Betty Callaway had erected. Never use four words when two will do, and never bare your soul because it's yours, not other people's.

When you get six 6.0s out of nine there is a great deal to say but only if you want to say it: and they had a problem. By upbringing, and from the solid stock, anything which smacked of boasting was A Very Great Sin and something they would not indulge themselves in. British reticence, Bulldog reserve, take it on the chin, stiff upper lip, all the clichés applied, everything all at once. Again this was not being misty-eyed. It was the truth.

And if you tried to tell the world about your six 6.0s how could it have sounded but boasting, however you phrased it? They were easily intelligent enough to calculate that and, if they hadn't, George and Betty Torvill and Colin and Betty Dean would have informed them, no nonsense. *We're not like that.*

It is a strength upon a strength upon a strength; and *Barnum* was still to come.

A Saturday afternoon, dusk early this far north, a dusk swallowing the last sharp winter sunlight which refracted through the rink's windows, pallid, ghostly, ethereal: a dusk which made the fierce lights illuminating the ice glow and glisten. Another air of anticipation, another place for it, the

same mood. Jayne caught that in the dressing room, sensed how many thousands were waiting just up there.

The 1984 Original Set Pattern was the Paso Doble. *It was stunning in its strident, almost savage climax* (Supersport).

They caressed the ice as they made their way to centre rink, he in white with a v-neck of coral blue sequins and a narrow black collar, she in white with a little neckband and a little waistband of coral blue. As they made their way she fashioned a sweeping-gesture with her right arm, a flourish: you're going to enjoy this. They positioned themselves, settled into composure, tranquility, raised their right arms and held them still. The music had not begun.

It opened with a fanfare. She hoisted her left leg and he caught it by the ankle, used that to propel her, pushing her along the ice so that — her right arm rigid ahead, her left leg still hoisted — she moved splayed and alone, immobile in body-gesture, only the width of a single blade maintaining her propulsion. He pursued her, caught the ankle again as the tempo of the

music increased We were into it, into *Barnum*.

She pivoted and he held her left leg in the palm of his hand, held the blade of her skate, used that as a fulcrum so that she leapt upwards, twisted in mid air and in a blurr landed somehow behind him but facing him. We were eight seconds into it, eight seconds into *Barnum*.

A spin sequence, he spinning her like a hoop, set the first of the applause and the applause didn't stop. It swelled as each circus trick followed, the juggling — she then he — the graphic and unmistakable portrayal of discarding juggles, the trapeze, their arms feeling out to maintain balance. Not overstated, understated. Crawford had made sure of that. They mimed putting the make-up on, mimed pulling on clowns' baggy pants.

He dipped his head and wielded the strength of his neck. She angled back onto him and he flipped her clean over using the neck alone, high, high, high. She landed crisp, clean, and the crowd threatened Gallic hysteria. That crowd rose in a cadence, the last of the winter sunlight melting

The victory complete, Torvill and Dean skate in the exhibition and leave the ice with a little bouquet-gatherer. She seems to be having a good time, too (Supersport).

through the windows. A garden of flowers cascaded from every direction and somewhere amongst it a thrown green teddy bear skittered across the ice. Christopher stooped, scooped it up and as they glided off he waved it, she peeking from behind a vast bouquet she'd garnered.

Every mark for technical merit — Torvill and Dean not yet in the arbour fringed with the fronds of shrubs — came up 5.9 and everyone knew that was only a prelude. A hush descended. Nobody coughed here, either; scarcely exhaled breath.

They stood, slightly breathless, Betty Callaway walking towards them, Michael Crawford next to her, the quadruple-act shoulder-to-shoulder. Their four faces turned towards the marks for artistic impression.

And the world went mad.

6.0 6.0 6.0 6.0 6.0 6.0 6.0 6.0 6.0

Christopher clasped both hands to his head, the teddy bear in one, the paw of a hand of Jayne in the other; her mouth opened so wide it wasn't a val-

ley but a canyon. Callaway permitted herself a smile, then forgot herself and danced up and down. Crawford screamed *Yes!*, punched the air, turned to them and screamed *Yes, Yes, YES!*, punched the air again. In those moments the quadruple-act, famed for self-control in public places, lost it and touched a million people, a hundred million, the more so because they did.

Soon after, and out of sight, Jayne Torvill burst into tears. The coming down from it was beyond mastering when it had happened. 'I felt miserable,' she'd say. Emptied.

As the fraternity departed Helsinki airport, an Arctic place where they spray the wings of the planes to de-frost them, everyone wondered how Torvill and Dean would follow *that* into the big finish, the Olympic year of 1984. Could they follow it? Could they force it on to somewhere else, another plateau, or would they take a step too far and fall off the mountain? Dare they force it? Dare they not? Questions, questions, questions. No answers. Just wait and see across the summer when they'd be in Oberstdorf.

Christopher already nursed ideas but was saying not one word.

Late autumn 1983 they sent word that the 'family' should gather on the day before the British Championships at Nottingham, but at the Stadium not the pub over the road. A grizzle-grey Midlands afternoon, the traffic ebbing and stuttering along the one-way system which uncoiled round the Stadium. Another ordinary Friday.

Maybe two dozen people sat in the rink, giving it a spooky this-is-a-private-occasion air. *What are you doing here? Still a voyeur after all these years?*

Yes.

Torvill and Dean had decided they'd unveil their free dance in a premeditated preview. They'd skate it and then answer questions about it. Other reasons for that this time. Christopher believed the free dance was so complex it would defy proper appreciation (and evaluation) unless you'd seen it at least once before the competition and heard his explanation of what it was and why it was.

He was not wrong.

The two dozen settled, and out on the broad ice Torvill and Dean, wearing billowing blue, sank gracefully and slowly and deliberately onto their knees and locked into one of their static postures.

No noise.

From all around *boomp-bubba-bubba-boomp-bubba-bubba-boomp* rose as a dawn chorus rises, pure and from nowhere, insisting you follow it, compelling your involvement, single beat multiplying onto single beat. A cur-

ABOVE LEFT Sarajevo, the 1984 Winter Olympics and the great, reverberating triumph. The compulsory dances were no trouble, no trouble at all (Supersport).

ABOVE RIGHT The arrogance of the Paso Doble. *Look at Christopher's face (Supersport).*

rent of a whisper flitted among the two dozen, mouth to mouth, murmur to murmur.

Bolero.

Mack and Mabel had expanded the confines but stayed inside them. *Barnum* stretched stretching further but stayed just inside them. Where to place *Bolero*? It left you bemused, critical faculties challenged and scattered, too much all at once.

The explanation came soon after. The cafeteria of such memory densely packed, overflowing, television crews — 'hey, we're *television*' — elbowing everybody out of the way, a brace of television questing-reporters firing questions from the hip and getting their sound bites, rat-a-tat. It's the wrong method with Torvill and Dean because they'll tell it the way it is if you give them enough space. Otherwise you have cleverly-constructed sound bites to pass a transient moment in a forgotten broadcast and what else would it be? Answer: a lot.

By now the persona had shifted. Christopher took the lead, Jayne nodding obediently and occasionally amplifying. He said 'It's for the judges to decide if we have taken a risk (with legality). It's not worrying us. It was difficult to find somewhere else to go after *Mack and Mabel* and *Barnum*. A

lot of people said we should do something similar, but each year we've tried to do something different. *Bolero* is a piece of music we have used for a long time for warming up, and it suddenly seemed right'.

He outlined the story, lovers overwhelmed by tragedy and throwing themselves in a volcano. Jayne did amplify that. 'We both die at the end' and then, terra firma. 'I have a permanent bruise on my knee from practising it.' She added that they needed to find a new way of breathing to cope with *Bolero*'s demands and, when they died on the ice at the end, they felt they *were* dying.

In my confusion I remembered that when I was a lad my father sat me down, put on a 78 rpm record of *Bolero* and said 'listen to this. It's the most monotonous thing you'll ever hear'. I offered that to Christopher in the form of a question. 'Aren't you worried about something so monotonous?'

'Monotonous?' he said, a lot crisper than a muse. He swivelled his eyes, settled them on me. His question was the answer.

Everybody is entitled to mistakes but I hope you, dear reader, never make one like this, one you'll listen to swelling and swelling until *Bolero* reduced strong men to tears and filtered into muzak for a country, difficult to *One of the instants so many people still remember and treasure during the* Paso Doble (Supersport).

escape, a temporary anthem; and bringing with it gold and gold and gold embossed on the fairy tale.

There was much else to savour in the competition before *Bolero*: the compulsories and a wish fulfilled with a 6.0 for the Rhumba, a galaxy of 6.0s for the OSP, the Paso Doble. They played matadors. This OSP, vivid and charged with dramatic choreography, excited the audience hugely, as it would continue to do. She wore a black cape, he black trousers, white top and epaulettes and, his chest thrust out, he strode down the ice dragging her behind him before he spun her onto the ice. Face down, she rotated and rotated. Composition: all 5.9s. Presentation:

6.0   6.0   6.0   5.9   6.0   5.9   6.0   6.0   5.9

Bolero was delicate as a bloom, sturdy as a bough, so slow in its unfolding, gesture woven into gesture, building, insisting, rising until they flung themselves into the volcano. Technical merit, all 5.9s. Artistic impression:

6.0   6.0   6.0   5.9   6.0   5.9   6.0   6.0   5.9

The deed done, Dean hovered waiting for a BBC television interview. He noticed me round the curve of the rink, sped over and said 'not bad for something monotonous'.

A couple of postscripts. Jayne's mother was still ribbing me about this 10 years later — 'you're the one who said that and we've often talked about it'. When my father died I searched his house for something I wanted very badly and found it — a faded green cardboard sleeve and inside a His Master's Voice 78 with, wreathed in gold lettering on its red label

BOLERO

(Ravel)

JACK HYLTON AND HIS ORCHESTRA

I have it still.

Budapest, 1984: already a city looking westward. The ruling communist party rode it on a light rein, right of travel long established and any business employing 30 people or less was private. You felt comfortable there, not surveyed.

The vast crowds which came to watch the Europeans at the rink on the rim of the city nursed an affection for Torvill and Dean through Regoeczy and Sallay. They nursed that affection because Torvill and Dean had trained

in Budapest so often: and if you were looking westward you'd perhaps respond more readily to Nottingham than Minsk.

By chance and improbability Sandra Elson was there as a competition helper. She'd married a Hungarian businessman. She moved around completely unnoticed until someone wondered who that stunning blonde speaking perfect English might be. Sandra Elson. Pardon? Yes, no mistake.

Torvill and Dean travelled smoothly through the compulsories, attracting 6,000 spectators, an amazing number for this stage of the competition. Only the Soviet judge — not Kabanov but a woman called Irina Absaliamova — marked Bestemianova and Bukin above them in the OSP. That stirred an uneasy current. The Soviets had been suggesting that parts of *Bolero* were illegal. Was that a warning shot?

The Paso Doble stirred the current too. In another direction, Bestemianova evidently hadn't been told about stone-faced Soviet inhibitions and volunteered that she'd watched Torvill and Dean in practice and found their Paso Doble 'so beautiful I could not free myself from the memory of it all day'. Absaliamova could.

The crowd acclaimed Torvill and Dean as they emerged onto the ice. The Paso Doble was a powerhouse climaxing in the arrogance of gesture when — chin jutting, chest thrust — he towed her along the ice, spun her down into the rotations. And up came 5.9s except the Czech and French (5.8) and the Soviet (5.6). The crowd hooted derision at that, whistled and booed. Presentation:

$$6.0 \quad 6.0 \quad 5.9 \quad 6.0 \quad 5.9 \quad 6.0 \quad 6.0 \quad 6.0 \quad 5.9$$

The 5.9s came from Italy, West Germany and You Know Who. Sallay described the 5.6 as 'disgusting' and couldn't believe it. Elson wondered if the Soviet judge could differentiate between a primary level foxtrot and a Paso Doble of this magnitude. Jayne said she was a bit 'surprised'. In the background a member of the Soviet party sought out Betty Callaway and apologised.

But: would the Soviets go public in questioning the legality of *Bolero*?

That Saturday afternoon the sheer size of the rink would give *Bolero* a new depth. The rink became an immense echo-chamber. During the warm-up session the ring Christopher wore on the middle finger of his left hand snagged a catch — one of the tiny metal rings you thread the laces through — on Jayne's boot.

He might have broken his finger and brought her down. They both

remained superstitious but after the warm-up he decided to remove the ring. 'I had never taken it off since my mother gave it to me on my fourteenth birthday. Frankly it was too dangerous to even think of leaving it on.'

Bolero's *full majesty holding a global audience of billions in a trance* (Colorsport *and* Supersport).

The seemingly trivial can magnify itself. Christopher did not permit that. When *Bolero* began, you felt in the presence of something momentous. There are sporting occasions like that but not many. They transcend competition and exist by themselves far above such mundane matters as gaining marks and getting medals.

The music encircled the rink in an embrace. Torvill and Dean reached out and held the rink in a caress. As with much great art, you need be no expert to understand it, and it came to you, you didn't have to go to it.

Mass surrender. *Bolero* proved so strong that a slight stumble by Christopher went unpunished and maybe largely unnoticed. Absaliamova was (surely) trapped in a private agony. She must have known what other judges would do. She faced The Fear Factor. Dare she risk marking Torvill and Dean down?

No.

Every mark for technical merit was 5.9 or 6.0. For artistic impression every mark was 6.0 except West Germany but that wasn't the end of it. At a press conference, Tatiana Tarasova, coach to B and B, launched a tirade. To gain the fury of it you need the background. Habitually *all* Soviet sportspersons in whatever guise offered platitudes and the tediously obvious ('we always aim to do our best'). The press conference began in an orthodox way, Tarasova speaking and the team's interpreter chugging along translating. The role of Eastern Bloc interpreters was never completely defined. Were they selected for diplomacy? Did they filter and sieve, translate the Party Line regardless of the real answers?

I happened to be sitting next to a Belgian woman, one of those unusual people who can speak a dozen languages. She hissed that Tarasova's answers were not being fully translated and started to do exactly that for me. She needn't have bothered. Tarasova's tirade centred on how high Christopher lifted Jayne during *Bolero* because beyond a certain height was illegal. Tarasova, fierce and formidable, insisted on making that point and to blazes with stone-faces, diplomacy, repercussions and the official interpreter. The words flowed in a torrent so passionate that the interpreter could only fol-

low on Tarasova's heels. Just this once we got the full, unadulterated version.

'Even as great a couple as Torvill and Dean should not violate the rules and I don't understand how they could allow themselves to do it. It is a bad example for all the others. We will not, however, protest. I don't think that is the right way do things.'

A stabbing question from the floor. *Your own judge gave Torvill and Dean 5.9 and 6.0. What about that?*

Tarasova, even more fierce and formidable when stabbed, drew on her considerable presence — she looked like the Kremlin in winter — and, brooking no argument, said 'I never comment on judges'.

The foyer of the hotel next to the rink later that afternoon: a broad foyer, the usual coming and going, the reception desk brisk and businesslike. Jayne stood encased in a white coat flicking open a pile of telegrams, reading each, passing to the next. Betty Callaway stood beside her. What about Tarasova's torrent? Mrs Callaway drew herself to her full height and asked 'do you want a statement for publication? After 16 years as a coach I am pleased the Russians have found a rule book'.

Lawrence Demmy, chairman of the international ice dance committee, offered a question of his own. *What do the Russians want — us to go out onto the ice with rulers and measure the lifts?*

Christopher, moving mildly on to the offensive, mused 'who do you listen to, Mr Demmy or a Russian coach?' But he did feel relief that the rhythm of *Bolero* had gained acceptance. Sarajevo and the 1984 Winter Olympics lay a month away.

Bolero continued to haunt me. The night of their win in Budapest four journalists, me among them, dined at the Forum Hotel on the banks of the Danube. Torvill and Dean arrived with Regoeczy and Sallay and took an adjoining table. It was one those awkward occasions when neither group wants to intrude on the other or to ignore the other. Pleasantries were exchanged.

A journalist (not me) thought it might be appropriate if the pianist, tinkling away in the corner, played *Bolero* in tribute. The journalist went over and, with a bribe of two gin and tonics, lured the pianist into tackling Ravel. As mistakes go, this was another big one.

The pianist tortured *Bolero* in an agony of noise, flat, limp and off-key, and of course it went on and on and on far beyond four minutes. Torvill and Dean were too sensitive and too polite to do anything except (mercifully) ignore us while we wriggled and squirmed. I kept imagining *they'll think it's me. I was the one who said Bolero was monotonous and now I've hired a*

pianist to prove it. The journalist went back and for a supplementary bribe of two gin and tonics persuaded the pianist to stop immediately. The silence brought tangible relief.

The Sarajevo harvest as the echoes of Bolero *melt. The Brits salute the Brits, Union Jacks everywhere* (Colorsport).

The meal over, Torvill and Dean left, handshakes and smiles and not a hint of a snide remark, not so much as an ironical quip. It's hard not to like such people. You spend your life writing about their mistakes and they're above mentioning yours.

Sarajevo today is a fractured spectre of a town, nightly on news bulletins with its bestial images of the middle ages. In February 1984 it lived peacably within the Yugoslavian confederation, cosmopolitan, flanked by snowy peaks, a Balkan cross-roads whose languages and buildings, churches and mosques, charted the tumult of its history. That history appeared to have settled into natural co-existence, no nuance of tension. The inhabitants, friendly and visibly proud to have an Olympics, prepared to be consumed by the delights of the Games: the Alpine ski-ing on a mountain called Bjelasnica, the bobsleighs on a mountain called Trebevic, the cross country skiers slogging it out at a place called Igman.

Paradoxically a Winter Olympics generates a communal warmth. It's

17. TORVILL J.
DEAN C.
GBR
ELEK
1 2 3 4 5 6 7 8
60 59 59 59 59 59 60 60

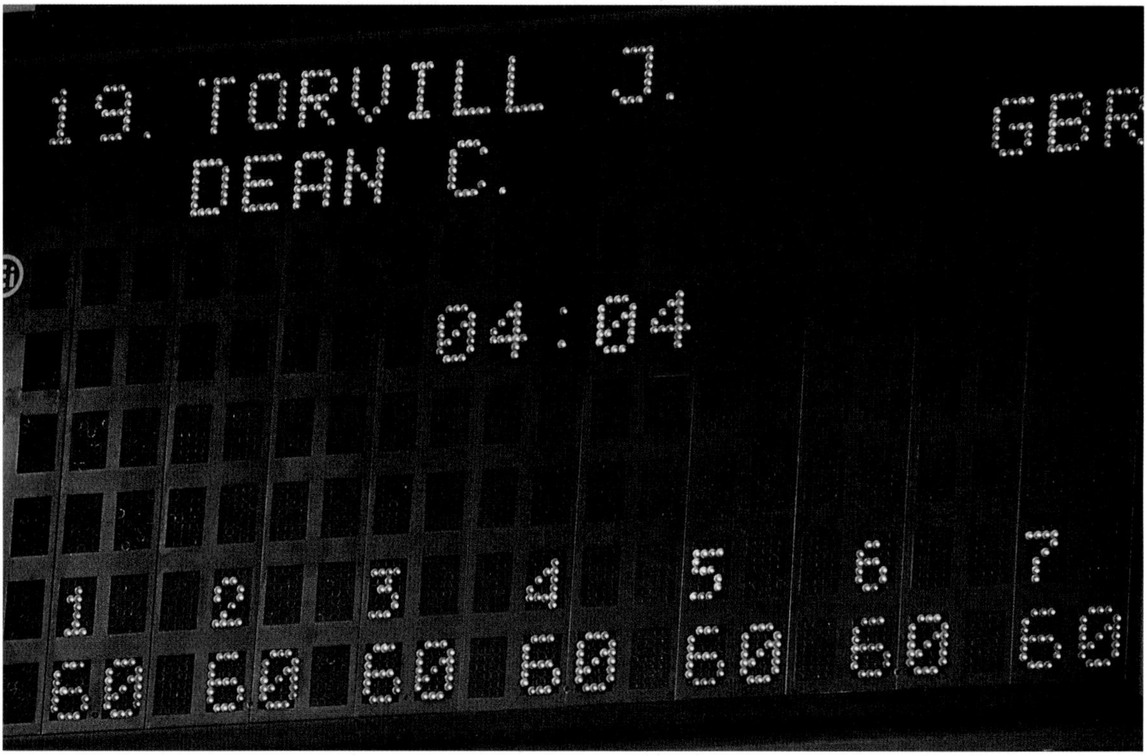
19. TORVILL J.
DEAN C.
GBR
04:04
1 2 3 4 5 6 7
60 60 60 60 60 60 60

smaller than the Summer Games, more matey and unbuttoned. It crosses all frontiers and for two weeks that February there were no frontiers in Sarajevo. Those are hard words to write now, when you don't know what fresh hell tonight's news bulletin will bring.

The greatest warmth would be spun at the rink called Zetra, a brief bus ride from the town centre. The macho men and brave women would contest the Alpine races, the never-give-up men and women contest the cross-country, the team-men contest the bobs, the fast men and women skim the speed skating, the bird men fly the ski jump.

None could be expected to cross all frontiers themselves, to touch a global audience: who cared about downhillers in, say, Sri Lanka? Who knew about bobs in, say, Central Africa? Who understood the marking of the ski jump in, say, Mexico?

Torvill and Dean were valid everywhere: handsome man and pretty woman who captivated because in their great art you truly needed to be no expert. And *Bolero* was a love story, and a love story is a love story in Sri Lanka and Central Africa and Mexico.

They journeyed late to Sarajevo. That allowed them to maximise their preparation in Oberstdorf. It kept the pressure at arm's length for as long as possible and the West German Skating Federation had laid on a special train to Sarajevo from Bavaria. Torvill and Dean hitched a ride. The sight of that train easing round a languid curve, then sighing into Sarajevo station of a chill, crisp morning seemed like The Real Arrival of the Games. Someone observed cryptically but accurately that *they* were with us now. It was Monday 6 February. The compulsories were on the Friday.

In between they presented themselves to the global media. Like with the Tarasova torrent, you need the background: a bowl of an auditorium, a table with Torvill and Dean behind it and a very persistent American television reporter poised to stab.

Fearing a media feeding frenzy Torvill and Dean had decided on this one press conference before the competition *and please would you leave us alone to concentrate on the skating afterwards? It's why we're here.*

Evidently the American had already tried for an interview and been refused. He fired from the hip. *Don't you have a responsibility to the global audience? Who are you to be so big that you're unreachable, untouchable? Where did all this high and mightiness come from?* Christopher explained patiently that if they tried to meet all requests they lacked the time to get on the ice. If they met some of the requests they'd be accused of favouritism. Hence this chance for anyone and every-

LEFT The two sets of marks which made history, three 6.0s for technical merit, a full house for artistic impression (Supersport).

107

one to ask whatever they wanted. The American fired from the hip again. *Maybe, but set piece press conferences don't make for good television. We want access to you on our terms, not yours.*

Christopher masked his irritation as best he could and we'd never seen a hint of irritation from him before. Then he bristled a bit and in the bristling increased stature. No sequined prancer, this. No. A man. Christopher said *you may be interested to know that we have not been speaking and will not be speaking to the British Press either. The rules are the same for all.*

The current of the press conference, their firmness in the face of hostility, revealed more about them than the usual run of ice skating questions. They were strong in their minds. They were ready. They retreated to the Olympic Village, which — like any Olympic Village — resembled a fortress with armed guards, a direct echo of the Munich massacre in 1972 when guerrillas broke in and murder was done.

The compulsories moved to a crescendo of three 6.os for the Westminster Waltz. Jayne, 'thrilled', felt they skated well but never thought of 6.os. They wouldn't leave terra firma and indeed touched it in the OSP on the Monday. At one point she put her hand on the ice, as staggering as Christopher falling in that warm-up at Copenhagen so long ago. A fleeting mistake, easy to miss if you were watching them from the wrong angle. They still received four 6.os. One reporter asked Jayne where her hand should have been and she replied curtly 'somewhere else' — the nearest to petulance we'd ever seen.

Re-enter the Americans. Princess Anne had arrived — she was President of the British Olympic Association — and, in congratulating Torvill and Dean immediately after they'd skated, attracted the photographers' feeding frenzy. While her congratulations were offered and gratefully accepted the competition continued, Blumberg and Seibert skating. One American ice dancer protested loudly *how did Blumberg and Seibert feel when every photographer in the place had their back to them? What about the noise all those photographers were making? Why didn't Her Royal Highness graciously meet Torvill and Dean somewhere in private?*

Princess Anne, who'd coped with such incidents regularly for a couple of decades, decided to dismiss any questioning. 'I'm not talking to any of you. Just take yourselves off.' Yes, ma'am. Nor were such incidents likely to disturb the mind-set of Torvill and Dean and they didn't. They'd skate the free dance the following evening, enough time away to forget such niggles and trifles as Americans bemoaning the fate of other Americans. Didn't they love our Royal Family? Evidently not that much.

A particular air of anticipation was born the next day, the Friday, reach-

ing into and across the whole town, touching everyone. *The faces of victory, joy and*
The context had been set now. By late afternoon, day- *tiredness mixed*
light softening into dusk, a black market for tickets (Colorsport).
developed outside the rink, very Balkan-looking touts
asking a month's wages in dinars for a ticket. The locals paid. If you can be
witness to something promising memories for a lifetime, why bother about
a month?

The final, climactic and decisive stage of a skating competition contains,
intrinsically, its own theatre, the lowly going first and laying the ground
for a gradual mounting of intensity. That this is interrupted because skaters
go in groups with warm-up sessions between each group increases the
intensity. The theatre constantly moves between action on an ascending
scale and the laid-back warm-ups where everybody, skaters, judges, officials, crowd, wait for the action to begin again. The final is a rack, not a
rush.

Layered over this that Friday night, the daylight gone now and the lights
from Zetra refracting out onto the hard snow caked round the approaches
to the rink, were two special kinds of presence. Princess Anne sat in atten-
dance among the British delegation bestowing, as royalty does, a certain
seal.

In that same crowd sat a phalanx of Russians, presumably members of the Soviet team in other sports but come to support Bestemianova and Bukin. They wore their brown fur hats and held their hammer and sickle flags and they decided to match the American phalanx in the crowd decibel for decibel. The Russians pitched camp opposite the Americans. They'd exchange decibels across the full width of the rink. In turn the two camps would make the rink ring: not taunt and counter-taunt but nearly. The British with their Union Jack hats and Union Jack flags sat circumspect.

Of the three couples in genuine contention for the gold medal — all of course the final group — Blumberg and Seibert went first after the warm-up. She, from Santa Monica, offered a sleek and frankly sexy presence, a wow of a girl; he, from Pittsburg, brought an elegance. In a moment or two they'd dug thundering approval from the American camp, *rah-rah-rah*, and the thunder fuelled the couple and the couple fuelled the thunder. Their programme lifted into the raunchy.

Torvill and Dean waited down the little stairwell from the dressing rooms, not watching. *Be strong enough to be yourself*.

Blumberg and Seibert conjured marks homing in on 5.8, greeted by a last thunderclap but leaving them vulnerable, too vulnerable. No nationalism and no chauvinism could mask that.

As B and B, the Muscovites, came on, the Russian camp waved their flags and sent thunder over to the American camp — already. Bestemianova: a slender dynamo, as if dissipating an enormous restless energy. Bukin: tall, sanguine, at moments seeming morose, the necessary foil as he stooped into her, held her, propelled her. When they'd finished a great quantity of bouquets were flung onto the ice.

Torvill and Dean waited down the little stairwell, not watching.

Bestemianova and Bukin had marks homing in on 5.8, creating and defining the last act, as the theatre would demand. Torvill and Dean had room to beat them but could afford no mistake.

They needed to be very calm then. As they prepared to skate, a tiny seven-year-old girl — Mirela Mornjakovic — one of those always on hand at competitions to help gather the thrown bouquets and thus clear the ice — still did just that, lifting the remains of B and B's harvest. Torvill and Dean waited a last time, steady, withdrawn far into themselves until Mirela completed her task, a billion or two televiewers round the world watching her, and skipped off back into anonymity.

They glided to centre rink, the British camp in seats half-held by shadow fluttering their Union Jacks in unison. They sank onto the ice, gave no impression of feeling towards the music for it to begin: weaved as it did,

that haunting beat gathering them up and transporting *Victory* (Supersport). them; they rose to it, wove into the great and gorgeous gestures, and they might have been in a trance, might have been hypnotising all witnesses from all camps. Time ceased. It might have lasted a handful of interlocking instants or an eternity. It lasted four minutes.

As they pitched themselves into the volcano Zetra rose, people up here, people there, everybody up cheering, flags of half a dozen nations waved. For this no frontiers existed. It had poured round the world and very suddenly it had ended. In the tumult he bowed, formal as you like — a courtly, courteous gesture — and she curtseyed, prim and neat, a gesture from a little girl's dancing class. Then he saw a woman at the rinkside with a bouquet and, lifting both arms to the crowd, went to receive it. Jayne drifted to other bouquets so that they hadn't had time to leave ice when the first set of marks came up. A shriek.

6.0   5.9   5.9   6.0   6.0   5.9   5.9   5.9   5.9

By now Jayne skirted the rink concealed by the bouquets she'd gathered and headed for more and more of them held over the rinkside. Christopher, nearby, continued to gather his own harvest. They came together and she accepted a final bouquet. They swivelled and set off on the journey to the

LEFT *In the Olympic Village the day after, natty, proper partners and now with gold medals* (Colorsport).

gate. They'd taken four steps when Jayne's face exploded.

6.0 6.0 6.0 6.0 6.0 6.0 6.0 6.0 6.0

She nestled her head into his shoulder, they turned in unison and waved a last time, he bowed, she bowed, and they tip-toed through the gate into the arms of Betty Callaway, who beamed: a very British thing to do. Princess Anne beamed too.

Some moments later Christopher came walking by, chaperoned by an official, and I sprang on him for a comment, any comment, which is what you do when the guillotine of copy deadlines hangs over you. I could summon only a reflex question. 'How did it go?'

He didn't break stride. 'All right.'

The ultimate devastating British understatement.

A few moments after that, John Hennessy telephoned *The Times* and a voice said 'there's not a dry eye in the country'.

4

And They Married Someone Else

A CAMEO, THE MONTH AFTER SARAJEVO, 1984. Torvill and Dean journeyed to Ottawa for the World Championships and an air of inevitability hung heavy over the competition. Nobody had the remotest hope of beating them and didn't — and the 6.0s flowed in a great torrent. There were seven for the compulsory dances, nine for presentation in the OSP, four for technical merit in the free, all nine for artistic impression. Truth to tell, Torvill and Dean found it harder and harder to express astonishment and disbelief at these marks. They did express delight, of course, but no person on planet earth with a television set could summon astonishment any more. Hence the inevitability. Could it have been a mere six years since Betty Callaway stepped into a lift in this same Canadian city and just about recognised a painfully shy policeman with a cold?

Ends and beginnings. With the World Championships over, they took part in the usual exhibition the day after. This exhibition, much loved by audiences, featured leading skaters doing special routines designed entirely to please. Some were hilarious (the Russians habitually uninhibited), some intriguing — one year three Soviet pairs did the same programme simultaneously, *six* skaters in perfect unison.

That last day in Ottawa, Torvill and Dean did *Bolero*, by popular demand, and an encore of *Bolero* — and the 11,000 audience in the rink wanted an encore to the encore. You could sense a communal sadness. *We won't be seeing anything like this again.* Torvill and Dean would turn professional, the path that leading skaters follow after the climax of their amateur careers.

After *Bolero* the plea for more swelled into a howl of demand from the 11,000. To satisfy the demand they skated a piece called *I Won't Send Roses*. You didn't need to know that (again) the story was of lovers torn apart, clinging to each other, torn apart again. Their gestures, their eyes, told you. Here was the cameo.

The piece unfolded like petals. In the quiet I began to hear snuffling, could see hands foraging for handker-

RIGHT *There would be no constraints when they turned professional. They could create whatever they wanted, and did* (Supersport).

114

chiefs. Then open sobbing began. A woman near me had tears streaming down her face and made no effort to stem them, simply watched, the gestures drawing her own emotions helplessly out of her. She couldn't bear to miss a moment. The depth of the story touched every heart. I wondered yet again: *what is this power that can be taken across an ocean, be expressed mute, and produce this reaction?*

It begged another question. If they could do it now, what would they do as professionals, with every constraint and rule removed? (Well, nearly removed. They'd compete in the World Professional Championships and win them although these championships — marked out of 10.0 rather than 6.0 — are in no sense comparable with amateur competition. They are regarded as an extention of show business.)

Their mums went to Ottawa, and we were on the same flight back, changing at Montreal. While we waited there for the connection we sat among Canadians who cannot possibly have known who Betty Torvill and Betty Dean were. Making sure the Canadians could hear, we ribbed the Bettys about *this Torvill and Dean, they seem promising and they'd probably be quite good if they practised harder.*

The Canadians eavesdropped and Betty Torvill's face creased into a wonderful, warm smile — you know, just like Jayne's. These people *are* the backbone of England, able to savour the irreverence as well as the great days. Mind you, Betty Dean responded. *Hmmm*, she said to me, *one of your eyebrows looks too long* — and plucked it out just like that. While I winced she burst out laughing, joined by Betty Torvill and the bewildered Canadians. Yes, good days as well as great days.

The fraternity dispersed and pondered, no doubt: 1985 and who would come through to replace Torvill and Dean. But many also pondered the big question. Where, suddenly and completely freed, would Christopher take the possibilities of human movement?

Torvill and Dean formed their own company and skated at Wembley Arena. So soon after turning professional, and in front of a home audience, they went through the repertoire from *Mack and Mabel* to *Bolero*. Before the show I asked Betty Callaway what they'd skate. The lot, she said. I expressed disbelief that, from a physical point of view alone, they could stand such an intensity on one night. Of course, she said — and they'll be doing other things too. Torvill and Dean, sprinters, covered a marathon that night.

They toured Australia and New Zealand, and worked *They made their first world tour in 1985. Here the cast is in rehearsal* (Supersport).

Naturally (and inevitably) people still wanted to see the Paso Doble *and its animal energy remained undiluted* (Supersport).

on an entirely new masterpiece. It was called *Fire and Ice* and it answered that big question. Recorded as a television special and released round the world on video, it contained lingering associations with *Bolero* but spread a feast into quite different dimensions.

Christopher became a ballet dancer across the opening sequence, set inside a volcano. A dozen other dancers, wearing little, undulated to throbbing music. Christopher glimpsed Jayne moving alone on ice, dreamlike, and he dived into a smoking cauldron to reach her. *Fire and Ice* rippled with a rich, luxurious montage of imagery: the molten, tinted red of the fire, the blue crystal-chill of the ice. Nor did it exclude the light touches. Christopher landed beside Jayne wearing ordinary footwear (well, large moccasins). Jayne tried to teach him to skate. He foundered, fell, slid on his stomach, rose, mastered it.

Fire and Ice contained many tender moments of that intimacy which *still* made you feel a voyeur. Perhaps a new audience, a show audience, wondered how that could be done without them being in love? It was the old question for ever renewed and still here. Not until years later did Torvill and Dean really answer this, during an interview with the *Radio Times*.

Jayne: 'At one stage, when we were adolescents, we were in love.'

Christopher: 'It's that boy-girl thing. There's something happening out there on the ice. It's to do with how we respond to each other. Viewers like to think there's something else. There aren't many jobs where a guy has to work with a girl in such a close way — touching, holding.'

Jayne: 'It's marriage without sex.'

A photocall for the first World Tour, a clutch of photographers capturing the most photogenic couple on earth and our photographer, Eileen Langsley of Supersport *capturing all of them.*

They were twice voted BBC's Sports Personality of the Year, taking the team prize in 1983 and the overall prize a year later. In 1983 a BBC producer, charged with booking them into a London hotel for the night, faced a delicate problem. One room or two? He could easily offend them either way, so he did what a man would do and asked Christopher. The reply — 'two rooms of course'.

The year of *Fire and Ice*, Christopher began to explore something which had always fascinated him: motor racing. The attraction to speed stirred 'slowly' because his first car, an Austin A40 which he bought for £70 with the help of a loan, wouldn't exactly thunder away from traffic lights, or

indeed from anywhere else. Reportedly it used as much oil as petrol. When he began to make money he graduated to an E-Type and a Porsche, but he wanted to race.

He received invitations to take part in celebrity events and that quickened his interest. He took single-seater lessons at the school at Silverstone, which you need to do because while you might think you're Nigel Mansell you must learn the mechanics of making a racing car perform: how to brake (always in straight lines, never in corners), where to brake for each corner, when to change gear (never in corners) and so forth. Single seaters are extremely sensitive. They twitch and spin easily. Neither E-Types nor Porsches do that even if you squeeze them hard. Twitching is designed out of them, and you have to *throw* them to spin them.

Christopher competed in some Formula Ford races. Formula Ford is affordable — neat little cars with 1600cc engines and the lowest rung on the big motorsport ladder. To launch his own career, Mansell went to the school at Silverstone and started in Formula Ford.

Of racing, Christopher would say 'It's a personal thing, just to be in tune with the car. When I'm skating I'm in tune with what my body's doing translated through the blades on the ice. Maybe you might be able to see your body as the car and the blades as the wheels'. The urge to race would have frightening consequences three years later.

In 1987 Torvill and Dean were guest stars with a famous American show company, IceCapades, and in 1988 made their second world tour, this time with skaters from the Soviet Union. It was an Olympic Year — Calgary — and Christopher had been coaching a French-Canadian couple, Isabelle Duchesnay and her brother Paul. The Duchesnays failed to make the Canadian team, and decided to skate for France. The two couples had known each other from training days in Oberstdorf and, as it seemed, the Duchesnays would be Torvill and Dean's natural successors. They had that quality which is so difficult to define — that creativity.

The fact that Christopher coached *foreigners* rather than British couples provoked a media flurry and one paper made it their main front page story. As it happened, I'd tried to reach Christopher about this — he was in New York — and typically he returned my call a couple of days later when he got the message. As I was out my daughter received the fright of her life. She picked up the receiver and a soft voice announced *Christopher Dean*. He was what he's been all his life (certainly within my hearing): charmingly polite.

A time was fixed for me to ring him at his hotel the following day, but I had a prior commitment elsewhere.

RIGHT Part of the programme or little Jayne having fun? Or maybe a bit of both? (Supersport).

I had to make the call from a public telephone box outside a railway station in Croydon — blessed be Phone Cards, but a peak time call to New York chews the units at a cosmic rate. Towards the end, the units melting, I had to ask him to speak faster. He did.

Christopher's argument: *I am as patriotic as the next man, but skating is international and art is international.* He left unstated the view which I hold. A skater of his extreme gifts would have little difficulty imparting the basics to others, or making others better, but a dozen coaches can do that. What he could surely also bring was an ability to mould the right material. He could, with a couple capable of responding to his thinking, lead and advise on the long journey towards at least the foothill of his own plateau. The Duchesnays looked the right material.

They put together a very Torvill and Dean free programme, but judges habitually marked it down in international competition. Was that because of the very name Dean associated with it, because the International Skating Union wanted to demonstrate that rules are rules and we're enforcing them? The ISU might have reasoned that *if we don't, the Duchesnays will continue the pushing of the frontiers and competitions will become meaningless. We'll have show skating in all but name.*

The marking-down produced another flurry. Ordinary folk responded to the Duchesnays in the same sort of way that they'd responded to Torvill and Dean, although on a lesser scale — and these same ordinary folk were both confused and confounded when the niggardly marks did come up. But that only brings us back to the web-like world of judging, and we've been there enough already.

In 1989, when they had finished touring with the Soviet skaters in Australia, Christopher accepted an invitation to race a souped-up production car on an oval circuit. He discovered that during a race the car in front punches a hole in the air, creating turbulence for the one following, and this has a direct effect on handling characteristics. (When Mansell tracked Ayrton Senna in the Japanese Grand Prix in 1991 Senna said 'I knew he was having a hell of a time behind me'.) Christopher's car went into a slide, headed towards a brick wall, and he thought, just as professional drivers do, 'this is going to be a big one'. He hit the wall and wondered if he had broken his legs. He hadn't, but his ankle hurt and his neck hurt: whiplash.

Such is the way of these things in the global village that a scrambled press agency flash message danced round the world, *Dean killed!* It was a Saturday. My telephone went hot from the *Sunday Express*, an excited voice saying

LEFT Contrast this with their Paso Doble the year before (Supersport).

ABOVE LEFT Smile, girl, smile — smile for eternity (Supersport).

ABOVE RIGHT The beginning of life without frontiers on the first World Tour, and a new set of stunning images (Supersport).

'Dean's dead'. As a long-time motorsport reporter I knew how strong modern cars were, how mercifully rare fatalities. I counselled extreme caution until the message had been substantiated and, sure enough, the thing scaled down of itself, to serious injury, to comparatively minor injuries. Subsequently I was able to rib Christopher about spoiling my Saturday morning, recounting the tale, and it amused him in a gentle, time-honoured way. *Reports of my death have been greatly exaggerated.*

Torvill and Dean toured the United States. There, a sound engineer from Chicago, Phil Christensen, was involved in the production. In January 1990 Phil, who Jayne described as 'tall and dark and handsome and charming', telephoned and asked for a date. She'd remember with her impish grin the romance of it: 'We went out to a McDonalds'.

ABOVE LEFT *In 1986, two years on, audiences still wanted the* Paso Doble *and got it* (Supersport).

ABOVE RIGHT *Going out to the world again in 1986, exploring Heaven and Hell. This is Heaven* (Supersport).

The question which Christopher had always parried — *Are you getting married?* 'Not this week' — would be answered. Jayne and Phil became engaged and a few months later married. Phil held an invaluable asset. He worked with Phil Collins and Genesis and understood the many aspects of public performing, understood that their work would keep them apart at times. When they announced the engagement they said the date of the wedding would be determined by their respective commitments, he on tour with Genesis, she in the States with the ice show. She insisted, however, that she would continue to skate with Christopher.

She revealed that she had been to Chicago to meet Phil's parents, and he'd been to Nottingham to meet hers, and 'they're very happy for me'. Christopher said 'Jayne and I are very close platonic friends. Hopefully now people will believe that'. Jayne said 'we still have a love affair on the ice every night'. To appreciate that homily you need to know all that had gone before: *it was only on the ice.*

That year, 1990, Torvill and Dean contested the World Professional Championships after an interval of five years, and won. They were elected American World Professional Skaters of the Year too. They remained big in Britain, even though they had been away for five years. When they opened a tour in Birmingham — doing a Rogers and Astaire *Top Hat* and

skating to music by John Lennon and Phil Collins — they outsold a Jason Donovan concert shortly before and, evidently, the whole tour outsold other recent tourers, The Rolling Stones.

Christopher outlined the new plateau. 'Performing in front of a live audience is never a routine thing. We can always make mistakes. Audiences expect us to be nothing less than perfect, but we demand that of ourselves as well.' He suggested that in future they might move towards smaller 'experimental' shows rather than the full blown extravaganzas. Little did he know.

Torvill and Dean remained big in all directions. During 1991 they toured Australia as guests of the South Australian Government. Domestically the BBC arts programme Omnibus made a documentary about Christopher's choreography. It attracted Omnibus's highest viewing and was repeated. Underlining their international appeal, the programme went overseas.

On the ice the Duchesnays, under Christopher's tutelage, finished second in the European Championships but won the Worlds in Munich. That year another romance blossomed — between Christopher and Isabelle. Christopher, by nature private and discreet, says it seemed right. They married in Canada. En route for the wedding, Jayne spoke of her own marriage, explaining that she'd put thoughts of having children to one side. 'We have our schedule set for the next few years, but after that, who knows?'

Christopher's marriage, which generated a brief media flurry when it failed, draws revealing comments from a seasoned journalist with the French daily sportspaper, L'Equipe. Alain Billouin covered athletics and the politics of the Olympics as well as the skating. I set this out because Billouin is perceptive. 'Whenever I saw Chris and Isabelle together, somehow I never had the feeling they were man and wife. I think he married Isabelle because Jayne got married.'

Billouin does not intend to imply that Jayne jilted Christopher because — without repeating the brother and sister comparison endlessly — we knew that, for at least a decade, no jilting would have been possible. They had excluded outside relationships under the imperatives of amateur competition and, while their professional careers also bore imperatives ('we make things tougher for ourselves on the ice all the time,' Jayne said) emotionally, they had long been free to marry whoever they wished. Moving into their thirties, they must have felt that marriages need not threaten the ice dancing partnership: it had frozen much too deep for that. Frozen solid. What Billouin does imply is that Christopher felt *if Jayne can marry, so can I*.

Torvill and Dean skated on.

Of the failure of Christopher's marriage, which happened fairly quickly — they divorced in 1993 — he says: 'We weren't compatible and should

This is Hell (Supersport).

never have married, but sometimes you don't see the realities until too late. She wanted me to help her career and thought it was time I gave up (the inference, give up touring). The minute someone tells you that you want to go in the opposite direction'.

Moreover, the Duchesnays suffered bitter disappointment in the 1992 Winter Olympics in Albertville when, representing France in France, they finished second. They retired. In time, Isabelle, announcing that their marriage had broken up, was reported as saying that Christopher had been unfaithful to her. There was another media flurry, but later she said she had been misquoted.

Far in the background of all this, the International Olympic Committee had changed their rules on amateurism, a step towards broadening the Games, and by implication tacitly accepting that true amateurism hadn't really existed for a generation. The IOC did not fling their doors open to allow payments or prize money, but they did class some professional sports as 'honorary amateurs' for the duration of the Games. It provoked initial

hilarity because the IOC admitted the megamillionaires of tennis, and tennis hadn't been an Olympic sport since 1924 in Paris. Tennis became an exhibition sport (a prelude to admittance) at Los Angeles in 1984 and came fully back at Seoul in 1988.

With the precedent set, the way opened to skating. In 1992 the International Skating Union invited Torvill and Dean to attend their centenary celebrations in Davos, Switzerland. Sitting on the train leaving Davos, Christopher turned to Jayne and said, 'Well, what about a comeback?' Jayne took that as one of his little jokes.

She said 'oh' and 'I really went quiet for a while'. It wasn't one of his little jokes. 'Then we both began talking about it a lot, how you'd do it, how you'd approach the work.'

Yet another Olympic change governed their thinking. This one involved time. By hallowed tradition the Summer and Winter Games took place in the same year at four-yearly intervals. The tradition reached back to 1924 when the Winter Games began. The IOC decided to break the cycle, making it two-yearly and alternating — Winter Games, Summer Games, Winter Games and so forth. To achieve this,

The company pose for the Press, obeying the dictum smile, smile, smile (Supersport).

they brought forward the 1996 Winter Games in Lillehammer to 1994, leaving the Summer Games at Atlanta in 1996. That re-set the cycle to go forward 1998 and 2000, 2002 and 2004 and so on.

If, Jayne confessed, Lillehammer had stayed at 1996 it would have put their return out of reach — she'd be 38, he'd be 37 — and they would have abandoned any notions of trying it. But the way the cycle had changed

The 1986 tour, redefining pageantry and always obeying the dictum of drama: it must have a centre of focus and take you with it, onward, upward, onward (Supersport).

'we felt the timing was right'. The year 1994 was not too far away, but far enough to give them time. They could examine their decision in minute detail and, if they decided to go for it, to relearn the lonely and iron disciplines of competitive skating. (Back to the dawn run or the late night shift?) They could practise and perfect what they would be required to do in competition, not just a free programme but to exercise their mastery over two compulsory dances and do an original dance, as the OSP was now called.

With a reputation the magnitude of theirs to defend, they saw the risks

writ large and would not undertake them lightly. They would spend 10 months weighing those risks. Any return in any sport after a decade has to be an awkward assortment of chances. A failure will diminish — even tarnish — the memory of what has gone before, not to mention that you will be *elderly* compared to those you will compete against — might look olde worlde and could make fools of yourselves. Torvill and Dean were never going to do that, but they measured themselves against exacting standards: the standards of, say, *Bolero*.

Meanwhile, they had a living to earn. They produced a new show for a British tour, described as a £10 million production. Some £1 million of lights illuminated Torvill and Dean, 60 Russians and Robin Cousins — a formidable gathering, everything all at once. One critic wrote that 'the stars are British with a breathtaking talent. Cousins performs with an infectious boyish grin, and Torvill and Dean are better than ever. Experience has added passion to the Paso Doble and *Bolero*, but now they truly dance in *Lo-commotion* and *Stormy Weather*'.

Without quibbling with this critique — the review appeared in *The Mail on Sunday* newspaper — you are entitled to wonder how much more passion could be added to the Paso Doble and *Bolero* than before. But it had been long ago, and memory slips and softens.

As we have seen, the careers of skaters are bisected in a unique way. The initial part, from humble and uncertain beginnings to championship excellence, is largely the province of the sporting media. Leading skaters, particularly if they are as good as Torvill and Dean, receive enormous and

regular publicity, hours of television at their national, European, Olympic and World competitions, and column inches stretching cumulatively for miles in the national and local press.

Only skating allows a second career in shows, because shows don't exist in any other sport. By the nature of the two careers, they are not only separate but different in character and scope; and the moment skaters do turn professional the volume of publicity alters and inevitably declines. They are into show business, and they will be getting the sort of reviews you have just read rather than *reports* of compulsory dances and free programmes, of the tumult and urgency of competition, of representing their country.

The professional tends to drift out of overall view, brilliant as a meteor shower at the occasional intervals when the shows play, then drift in again — to New York, to Melbourne, to who follows where? Precisely this hap-

Trenary in action during the Winter Olympic Games in Calgary, 1988 (Supersport).

pened to John Curry and in turn to Cousins. Someone once asked me where Cousins was living these days and I had no idea. I hadn't had any occasion to talk to him for four years. I had reported every move of his competitive career, hung on the agonies and ultimate triumph of that, seen his first professional show — and then he was gone. To his parents in Bristol, to New York, to his favoured rink in Denver, who knew? That's the way it goes.

I set out this context because Torvill and Dean remained box office. They remained a presence in everybody's memories, re-invigorated via their shows and their television specials — however sporadically — but who knew where they were or what they were doing beyond that? Motor racing in Australia? Working with the Bolshoi? Living in England or New England or neither? No reporters tracked them daily now, and hadn't for close on a decade. No Olympic medals were in play, no cold wars had to be fought and won.

If you understand this you will take in the full impact of the decorous events at the Royal Albert Hall, London, one seemingly ordinary winter's day.

5

The Risk of Their Lives

'WE ARE DELIGHTED TO WELCOME CHRISTOPHER AND JAYNE, who really need no introduction. As you will have realised by now, later in the proceedings they will sign the necessary papers to return them to the eligible status required to compete in international championships again. Their application will go forward to the International Skating Union's meeting in June. Christopher and Jayne will receive our whole-hearted support in every possible way.'

The gently aristocratic intonations of Courtney Jones, President of the British National Ice Skating Association and a former world ice dance champion, seemed almost sonorous — no particular emotion — as he made the announcement in a side-room at the Royal Albert Hall. It was as good a place as any for the announcement — central and imposing.

This was March 1993.

Christopher and Jayne, sitting on either side of him, looked particularly relaxed, plucked all at once from memory. Could it really have been a decade since Sarajevo? Time had touched them lightly. He looked more Foreign Office than ever. Her face had filled out but, moving through her emotions, the child-girl-woman image lingered — it was a merry, twinkling face, a conductor of light.

Such is the way of the world that whispers of the comeback had grown into firm stories days before, rendering the announcement something of a formality. That did not lessen the sense of occasion. While a dozen cameras craned and clicked, they put the application forms on the table and signed. Betty Callaway, next to Christopher, watched intently. That done, the questions began.

Could you talk us through the reasons?

Christopher: 'When we turned professional we thought we wouldn't consider coming back. I think every skater says that the moment they turn professional. It wasn't an option for us anyway. Then, when the ISU opened up the possibility, we thought we'd come full circle on ourselves in the performances and the shows that we do.

The return, older now and yet somehow the same. They'd face the journalists and explain what motivated them to come back but wouldn't say a word about their free programme – yet (Supersport).

It seemed right. It gives us a new lease of life almost'.

Who mentioned it first?

Jayne: 'I think Chris mentioned it to me and I thought he was joking. When the time came where we really did have to make the decision, we thought about it more seriously. Because the Winter Olympics were now to be in 1994, it became an opportunity that we didn't want to miss. We are still allowed to do professional shows but, in fact, we don't because we need to spend all our time training'.

What possible fresh challenge can it offer you?

Christopher: 'Going to the Olympics and competing at the forefront of skating again. It was something we felt we had been very much a part of. Through our professional life we have developed, learnt more, matured. We still believe we have the ability, and we love to go out and perform. At the end of the day we're exhibitionists. It's part of us and it's something we want to do, to be out there in front of an audience performing'.

People may say you're an automatic for the gold in Lillehammer. Is that how you see it?

'No.'

Jayne (quickly): 'No. We would never be that complacent. Many things can happen. We know there are a lot of good skaters today so we'll have strong competition. We intend to work hard'.

Betty Callaway says you're better than when you stopped as amateurs.

Jayne: 'We hope we've improved, but of course the standard of skating has improved. We feel we've kept up with that, pushed ourselves even further. We'll see'.

Did you do any genuine soul-searching about the risk of failing?

Christopher: 'Every hour of every day'.

Jayne: 'We decided to be positive once we made the decision. We try not to think about the other things and we'll get many questions — "do you think you'll win?" — but we'll ignore them and concentrate on the skating'.

Christopher: 'When we left it, we left it at a very high point and our image seemed to be very high as well. The expectations will be the same. People will obviously be looking for anything under par, or anything

The team of '94: Bobby Thompson, a creative force in ice dancing, Torvill and Dean and their smiles, smiles, smiles, Betty Callaway, the calm sage (Supersport).

slightly less than we were. We had to consider if we felt we were still good enough to compete in that way. Obviously by the decision we believe we can mount a strong challenge. So we've done it'.

You must have seen the opposition?

Christopher: 'Yes, yes. Very strong opposition and very talented, as it always has been'.

Is there any longer any meaningful distinction between professional and amateur?

Christopher: 'It's changing and the two are much closer together. To compete, you have to be practising all the hours that you can possibly practise of all the weeks and days you can put together. The difference is that one is paid, and the other's paid in a different way. Competitive skating is certainly heading in a more open direction'.

Don't you feel uncomfortable at the rather contrived way you are being allowed to put a foot back into the amateur camp?

The return, still charmed and charming, Jayne still somehow the child-girl-woman although married now (Supersport).

Christopher: 'I don't think it's contrived. What the ISU and the IOC recognised was that if they want the best in the world they had to open it up to people who had become professionals'.

The tennis players in Barcelona wouldn't stay in the

Olympic Village. Do you expect to stay there and generally muck in?

Jayne: 'The Olympics is a special event and you get caught up in the whole thing anyway. We'll be there if we're chosen'.

Are you too old to compete against youngsters?

Jayne (chuckle): 'I'll race them up and down stairs'.

Christopher: 'Also we have the maturity as well, as opposed to single skaters'. (Solo skaters need more overt athleticism, leaping into triple jumps.)

Every year between Innsbruck 1981 and Bolero was a distinct step. Where do you go now?

Christopher (deep chuckle): 'Well . . .'

Jayne: 'We obviously have to come up with something far better than anything we've done before. We'll be doing a lot of thinking and listening to try and come up with the right thing. We have some ideas at the moment but nothing definite'.

What do you think of the restrictions imposed in ice dance now?

Jayne: 'There had to be restrictions to keep it to the point where skaters can be judged. Because we've been professionals we've had absolutely none, and now it's a challenge. We have to conform'.

Jayne's husband Phil Christensen attended but kept in the background, approachable, easy in the American way. 'I've worked with their shows as well as Genesis. I sort of split my time last year between them,' he'd say. Questions reared at him.

When they were skating before, they were extremely close. Both are married (Dean was not yet divorced). How might that affect their skating?

'If you go watch them train you'll know, as I'm sure you do know, that when they get on the ice it's television. I suppose it's like anybody else: when you're really into what you are doing you concentrate on it. They are, for all that I know about ice skating, the best I've ever seen. When I see other couples or individuals train — for instance in shows — they go out for half an hour, go round a few times. Every day Chris and Jayne go through every move that they've done wrong the night before, and they fix it for the show that night. I'm sure they will in competition'.

Can they go on doing that now they're married? Isn't the amount of time they can spend together restricted?

'Not really. I mean, in the past, even with tours that's very concentrated, it's a lot of their time. I suppose one has to make sacrifices for what one wants, and it's something they do really want. So we all make compromises.'

You've been with them on their tours. Isabelle not.

'Isabelle Duchesnay is a skater in her own right with her brother, and they do their own shows. They are very popular, so there is no reason for them to come onto another person's show. I think that's why Isabelle hasn't actually performed in a Torvill and Dean show. But I'm sure Isabelle would be very supportive of Chris.'

What do you do with Genesis?

'My speciality is the sound on stage. Chris and Jayne choose their own music. Obviously we all buy music and listen to music and if anything comes from that well and good, but I don't foresee getting involved in the comeback. This is their world. I'm not a musician. I'm not an arranger. I'm not a composer. I don't see what I can do except say "Gee, that wasn't a very good recording".'

Are they excited about the comeback?

'Excited? They took a long time to make the decision and they feel very confident. They don't have big heads, they don't say "Oh, we're just going to win". They say "We're going to go in and do the best we can".'

Later Christopher sits in a corner of the side-room for a more intimate question-and-answer session, although before I can say a word he wonders if I've 'come straight from São Paulo' and the Brazilian Grand Prix. I explain that Torvill and Dean are priorities again, and while I admire Ayrton Senna (who won) enormously, this is the place to be. He smiles. I say 'I'm coming back with your comeback and when you go away again I'll go away again, you know, like the time before'. At that Jayne laughs out loud.

She reveals that she's undergone a bone-shaving operation on her foot, and 'I hope I don't need another. I hope that's it. It's fine. It occurred at the beginning of the last tour but I couldn't have the operation till I'd finished the tour. I had to wear protective support'.

You are married but you weren't before. You were able to focus totally on the skating. Will you be able to do that?

Jayne: 'We have been focused since we married, because any time we're working on tour or for our own show we take ourselves away as we did before, we go into isolation — but even more so in this case. As soon as we start our preparation we'll isolate ourselves'.

Will the relationship with Christopher be the same?

Jayne: 'It doesn't really matter. We've known each other for so long — so much longer than we've known our respective partners in life — and when we've a job to do we know how to approach it'.

Has it taken pressure off you that endless people don't ask when you'll get married?

Jayne (merrily): 'There'll be another question we'll be asked every time. We don't know what it is yet'.

Like when are you going to be pregnant?

Jayne (clucking): 'Probably'.

Christopher: 'What about that time-clock, Jayne, ticking away?' (She was 35.)

Jayne: 'Oh dear'.

And this comeback?

Jayne: 'We talked about it in the full circle — "Oh, wouldn't it be great?" to "Oh gosh, what have we done?" — and came to the view that there are more positive things in it for us than negative'.

Christopher: 'In a sense, 10 years down the road, we felt what's left for us? What stimulant? We're sort of on a downward slide, and suddenly someone opens up a whole new ballgame'.

Jayne (raising her voice): 'Yes, yes. When it's your own show you can decide what you do, but we've certainly not had any easy shows. They have always had a challenge within them and very hard physical pieces for us.

By now they'd entered the International Skating Union's Hall of Fame although, strictly speaking, they'd been there a long time (Supersport).

We feel we are always pushing ourselves one way or another, and we think we are better skaters'.

Christopher: 'We'll start our preparations the minute our tours end in June. That gives us about six months before the British Championships'.

And so it continued, spawning question after question the way it had been that other time. What would they create for the free dance? How would they cope with the externally enforced discipline — the regulations? Moreover, the composition of ice dancing had changed: two compulsory dances instead of three, the OSP (original set pattern) renamed the original dance, and a proviso lurking around the free. The received wisdom, early in 1993, appeared to be this: the ISU insisted on traditional ice dancing, which might hem and hamper Torvill and Dean's freedom of movement. What would they dare? Challenge the ISU with something like *Fire and Ice*? Go orthodox? (I tried to lure Jayne into a trap long after the Albert Hall by asking what the music was, hoping to catch her off guard. Small chance. She grinned enigmatically and let the moment go. Nothing had changed.)

The British Championships at Sheffield, January 1994, and Torvill and Dean capture the mood perceptively the day before, giving this to the photographers (Supersport).

They practised at the rink at Milton Keynes, handy for both of them. They enlisted Betty Callaway and Bobby Thompson, a former national team coach and long a friend, to advise. And they practised in secret. No doubt an intrepid journalist could have gained admission to the rink on some pretext some forgotten morning and watched, but that would have been more than a betrayal of trust. That would have been like a publisher putting the name of whodunnit on the jacket of a whodunnit. Better to savour the suspense, the way it had been with *Mack and Mabel* and *Barnum* and blessed *Bolero*.

Early January 1994. They conducted the unveiling at the Sheffield Arena the day before the British Championships, a championship which attracted a major sponsor, People's Phone. No doubt the presence of Torvill and Dean helped. Christopher said there didn't seem much point in delaying the unveiling any longer.

ABOVE LEFT Sheffield, 1994 and the mastery of the intricacies of the compulsory dances hadn't gone away. The innate elegance remained, potent and precise (Supersport).

ABOVE RIGHT The Rhumba, Sheffield: languid as Summertime Blues *had been all those years ago, sensuous, profound and without question a masterpiece in the great tradition* (Supersport).

Let's Face The Music And Dance.

Not Ravel, no, Irving Berlin. It drew memories of Ginger Rogers and Fred Astaire, but Christopher stressed they weren't inviting comparison with that particular partnership. 'The piece takes us back to social dancing, to the rhythms of the ballroom — foxtrot, waltz and tango — with a couple of surprises. We've known the music for a long time, but it was a question of finding the right vehicle for it. We believe it is the way the ISU wants ice dancing to go.' That was the received wisdom.

The countdown to the comeback proved a time-warp of its own.

Christopher: 'Fifteen weeks ago I said to myself "The Championships are getting close and we aren't getting close to it" ', to which Jayne added that it had come upon them in a strange and urgent compression, from a long time left to only weeks left, to no time left, to now.

Jayne: 'There are so many steps that when we were first doing it we found it hard to remember what to do next! It is the most demanding piece we've ever done'. She made a direct comparison with *Bolero*: if you distilled all the moves in *Bolero* they would represent only the first minute of *Let's Face The Music*.

Thompson was visibly in thrall to it and couldn't disguise that. It is, he insisted, the most difficult skating ever attempted anywhere by anybody. Callaway fielded the inevitable question — are they as good as before? — by erecting her shield. Nothing had changed. *They're better*, she said, as she'd said at the Albert Hall.

Christopher estimated that to compete as amateurs cost them £100,000 ('well, we won't get much change out of that') in expenses and loss of earnings.

The fascination of their relationship remained. Jayne felt it helped that she was married and Christopher — now divorced — had a life of his own. Over the past few years they had made space for each other, and sometimes it was good to go their separate ways in the evening, switch off from it, return to the rink next day refreshed. They socialised, but through choice rather than necessity.

They had grown up.

They found the practising a bit eerie, *having* to go to an empty rink of a morning, but they established a routine, a method of working, and for long moments it felt as if they'd never been gone.

And so they returned, to the expanse of Sheffield Arena. Torvill and Dean moved on to the ice for a photo call, skimmed along with a Union Jack billowing behind them. When they were ready they did *Let's Face The Music*. Nothing had changed: you needed time and repetition to digest what it offered; you needed to consult the technical experts to be sure of the extent of its complexities. Any fool could see it was complex. Only the expert can quantify the degree.

The first impression: a curious ambivalence. It was like watching a pianist's fingers rippling in a masterly and controlled cadence, each key perfectly touched as no other pianist on earth can do, but it didn't demand that you were on your feet at the end, transported by the music to a place beyond yourself. You were still admiring the fingerwork. Mind you, after my own performance with *Bolero* I was ready to keep my mouth shut, my horizons open and let the judges decide.

That evening the draw for the skating order was made in a Sheffield hotel. Christopher exercised his considerable charm to chat to anyone who ventured up to him. Many famous people seem forbidding to the stranger, the reputation preceding them. Christopher has never been like that. Conversation with him is easy. Weeks before, we'd talked about this and that, and I mentioned I was writing a biography of the Ferrari driver Gerhard Berger (published by Patrick Stephens Limited). Christopher wanted to know all about the horrific and fiery crash Berger had in a race in 1989, what was I writing about that, what had I found out? He understands his motorsport, and was present at Silverstone the race the crowd invaded the circuit to salute Mansell before the British Grand Prix finished. He didn't invade the circuit, of course. All else aside, he's not the kind.

That Sheffield evening I'd taken another of my racing books for him as a present. I gave it to him when the draw had been made: a quiet corner of the hotel, he holds hands with Jill Trenary, Jayne and Phil sit on a sofa, Betty Callaway is there, a cosy atmosphere, and a bit of banter. While the banter passes to and fro Christopher is already peeking into the book . . .

The first compulsory, the Starlight Waltz, involved a mandatory 32 steps in a pattern. The ease, elegance and precision, the essential smoothness of Torvill and Dean had not deserted them, and their marks averaged 5.7. The second compulsory, the Blues, was nothing like *Summertime* but threaded through with that ease again, the marks averaging 5.8.

The original dance, the Rhumba, equalled anything they'd done before, a masterpiece for the long gallery. They took it as slowly as the rules permitted, drawing sensuality from it, eyes locked on to eyes, provocative gesture balanced against provocative gesture. Only one judge marked them

lower than 5.9 for composition — and for presentation up they came:

The deceptive moment at Sheffield, all 6.0s again and the world seemed ripe for re-conquest (Supersport).

6.0   6.0   6.0   6.0   5.9   5.9   5.9   5.9   5.9

Had it really been a decade? After the first set of marks Jayne leant over and tickled Bobby Thompson's chin, but as she waited for the second set you could see tension in her face. That dissolved as the score-board blinked out the 6.0s and she patted Christopher's hand, smiled and smiled and smiled, waved to the crowd.

The Saturday of the free, Betty Torvill sat in one of the stands. Dad George had been the day before to see the unveiling and when Jayne asked him what he thought, Betty reported, George had said 'not bad'. Yes, keep your feet on the ground, see it in perspective.

Let's Face The Music became an enigma. They went first after the final warm-up. She coughed to clear her throat, he looked benevolently at her, part reassurance, part *let's do the business*. They exchanged a couple of words. He took a deep breath, exhaled, and she put her smile on. They moved to centre ice and began. At the first modulation of tempo — from slow to semi-quick — the hand clapping to the rhythm ought to have risen

from the 8,000 crowd but it didn't; nor did feet stamp either. Maybe the piece pitched the 8,000 too suddenly into something of such a scope that they had little idea how to react.

Afterwards they sat in the familiar, time-honoured arbour, the fronds of potted shrubs as a backdrop, the television camera viewing every dewdrop of sweat. He put his anorak on. Technical merit:

$$5.9 \quad 5.9 \quad 5.9 \quad 5.9 \quad 5.9 \quad 5.9 \quad 6.0 \quad 5.9 \quad 5.9$$

A brief pause before the artistic impression — then the world went mad again.

$$6.0 \quad 6.0 \quad 6.0 \quad 6.0 \quad 6.0 \quad 6.0 \quad 6.0 \quad 6.0 \quad 6.0$$

She clasped him round the neck, but her face changed as they stood to salute the crowd. She turned to him and she was crying before her head reached towards the comfort of his shoulder. She clasped a paw of a hand to her eyes and sobbed like a tiny girl, shook her head: everything all at once, a releasing of tension that they got through it, the great risk vindicated so far.

The familiar configurations of conquest, Jayne surrendering to the emotion of it. An instant later she'd be in tears of relief (Supersport).

Jayne said that 'seeing the set of marks made me very emotional. It was a nice feeling and I didn't think we could have done it any better. We were nervous and apprehensive. It was like a replay of the 1984 Olympics. It was also important for us to show this routine in competition, and the marks give us confidence for the build up to the Europeans. Now we have done at competition level again — 10 years is a long time — we will be more relaxed. We felt a lot of pressure, and it was not a formality'.

John Hennessy of *The Times* suffered something akin to agonies trying to find the right context to describe *his* ambivalence. He wrote how the gallery of masterpieces had touched him, but after *Let's Face The Music* 'I felt a desperate emptiness'. The phalanx of 6.0s did not alleviate Hennessy's plight or mine. Among the fraternity there were divisions, some adoring it, some nursing doubts. The popular press entertained no doubts and gabbled of the golden couple, miles of column inches in that strain. Some of the fraternity echoed that, complicating the finding of the context.

I'd have felt easier in myself if the 8,000 had sent their blessing and their appreciation with a drum-beat of feet and hands, swamped the rink in sound, made the championship into the sort of celebration we'd known so many times in so many places.

Time tightened. When the British Championships had been in late November it allowed some six weeks to work on the evolution of a free programme, which is what happened with *Bolero* in 1984. Sheffield finished on Saturday 8 January, the Europeans in Copenhagen began on Tuesday 18 January: only long enough to catch your breath, recuperate, do a bit of work and find your way to Heathrow.

In Copenhagen, where *Mack and Mabel* had stirred a thunderous drum-beat 12 years before, Torvill and Dean faced the World Champions Maia Usova and Alexandr Zhulin, who had been training in laboured secrecy in Lake Placid and whose free dance no-one had seen. The other, precocious, pretenders were Oksana Gritschuk and Evgeny Platov. The cold war was on again and only the generations changed.

Arriving there, Christopher admitted to 'changes since Sheffield, subtle changes' and chose not to elaborate. In training, neither Russian couple showed their full free programmes but offered tantalizing glimpses. Gritschuk and Platov would do Rock 'n' Roll and the glimpses suggested the sort of reaction Torvill and Dean once conjured: lift an audience up, set it down again.

The psychology of a championship remained the slots, even at the summit, although it was more fluid now. The slots weren't set in ice, so to speak, and couples might recover from a moderate start — but historically the couple who won the first compulsory tended to win the champi-

onship. Torvill and Dean were third after that first compulsory, the Paso Doble, with a mark as low as 5.2 from the Swiss judge. Jayne said she didn't think they could have skated it better. Ominous.

After the Blues they drew level with Gritschuk and Platov, second equal to Usova and Zhulin. The psychology became important for two reasons. Torvill and Dean had led after every section of every competition since Innsbruck, 1981. The judges seemed to be saying Torvill and Dean are no longer infallible, invincible, immortally perfect. It left them vulnerable, something else they had not known since Innsbruck.

At this point Betty Callaway stepped into the cold war. She mused that, in the Blues, Usova and Zhulin didn't do one step correctly, and of the judge who gave them 5.9 she added pointedly 'that means close to perfection. Ridiculous'.

In the original dance, Usova and Zhulin hammered marks of 5.9 to 5.8 for presentation. That set the standard. Torvill and Dean uncoiled to their Rhumba. At the moment when they thrust their faces close and were poised to kiss, the applause did rise, and rose again during the step sequence. What would the judges do? Composition from 5.9 to 5.5 (the Austrian judge). That got cat calls, proper derision, shrill hooting. Up they came for presentation:

5.9   6.0   5.9   5.9   6.0   5.9   5.9   5.8   5.9

In order these marks were given by Poland, Britain, Estonia, Germany, the Czech Republic, Switzerland, France, the Ukraine and Austria. It meant Torvill and Dean were first equal with Usova and Zhulin, everything turning on the free.

The order of skating assumed a particular importance, the couple going last enjoying a theoretical advantage. That was Gritschuk and Platov. Nothing had changed. The judges needed to leave themselves room for manoeuvre as one couple followed another. They could not give any couple but the last unbeatable marks in case the last couple were better.

The psychology of the final group's warm-up: Torvill and Dean had withdrawn into themselves, not noticing the Russians who floated by, or choosing not to notice. No eye contact, nothing — moves and countermoves in the cold war, shadow boxing, mind games and so beautifully executed it might not have been that at all. *You're reading too much into it, we weren't doing that, we were just doing our own thing.* As the warm-up ended the couples cleared the ice decorously, leaving Usova and Zhulin composing themselves. They'd go now. They had the drum-beat beating back to them after only a few steps, and they looked ominously good — fluid, exciting, the calibre of champions, that pedigree you can't mistake. Technical merit:

5.8   5.7   5.8   5.7   5.7   5.7   5.8   5.9   5.7

Maybe the marks for artistic impression might offer Torvill and Dean, next to perform, some room for manoeuvre. They did, but not much:

5.9   5.9   5.9   5.8   5.9   5.8   5.9   5.9   5.9

A shriek greeted Torvill and Dean — born of affection, nursed by expectation? You didn't know what impulses moved this immense crowd. The drum-beat did rise, hands beating, and profound applause — a completely different sound — as the crowd drank deep of the moods and movements

of the piece. *Let's Face The Music* got itself a standing ova-
tion. Technical merit:

5.7   5.9   5.8   5.8   5.7   5.8   5.7   5.8   5.8

The marks for artistic impression would be the pivot,
the fulcrum. A 6.0? A galaxy of 6.0s? No.

5.9   5.9   5.8   5.9   5.8   5.9   5.9   5.9   5.9

Usova and Zhulin had so far beaten them by five judges to four. Christopher
looked wearied, the smile by rote. He shook his head, clutched a small bottle of mineral water, stood, moved off towing Jayne in his wake.

Next: Gritschuk and Platov, rocking 'n' rolling, convulsing the rink, a
saxophone striking out the beat. The Rock 'n' Roll became an event. Elvis
the Pelvis reincarnated, a happening, wild and tamed, raw and refined,
everything all at once. Torvill and Dean were in their changing rooms.
Technical merit:

5.9   5.9   5.9   5.9   5.9   5.9   5.8   5.8   5.9

That was a prelude, a feel towards a consummation, and a sense of that

hung heavy over the Brondby-Hallen, Copenhagen, in the few seconds until the artistic impression:

6.0 6.0 5.9 6.0 5.9 5.9 5.8 5.8 5.9

Gritschuk burst into tears. Did she realise she'd altered everything? Probably not. The conclusion of the European Skating Championships in January 1994 belonged to Mensa and micro chips. A BBC producer, downstairs near Torvill and Dean, wore an earpiece to stay in touch. The computer spoke, a message was relayed and the producer shouted 'We've done it!' Jayne Torvill did not understand how. Christopher Dean did not understand how. Perhaps only a dozen people on earth did. It baffled the whole of Britain, who understood them to be holding no more than bronze medals.

So how did Torvill and Dean win?

BELOW LEFT It was good, technically it was so demanding you couldn't absorb its scope easily, but the judges thought it wasn't good enough for gold in Copenhagen. By a quirk it won (Allsport).

BELOW RIGHT However you get there you're on the top rung of the podium and nobody can make you step down. The Olympics were merely a month away . . . and would Let's Face The Music *survive there? (Allsport).*

It is not as complicated as it sounds, and however strange the marking, it has a certain logic. If you keep in mind two things you'll find your way through the maze: (1) the judges' marks are *only* the way of establishing the finishing order, as we've seen before; and (2) because the free dance carries such a heavy percentage of the Championship's total marks, whichever finished in front of the other in the free — Torvill and Dean, or Usova and Zhulin — *had* done it. Going to the free, Gritschuk and Platov were too far behind to be anything but spoilers.

These are the steps. The figures show successively where each judge positioned the couples in the free after each had skated:

Usova, Zhulin	1	1	1	1	1	1	1	1	1

Torvill and Dean then did *Let's Face The Music* and all seemed lost because the judges gave these positionings:

Usova, Zhulin	1	2	1	2	1	2	1	1	2
Torvill, Dean	2	1	2	1	2	1	2	2	1

Torvill and Dean had apparently lost because only four of the nine judges put them at 1, five judges put the Russians at 1, a straight defeat 5-4. Now enter the spoilers Gritschuk and Platov with their army of 5.9s and 6.0s to give these positionings:

Usova, Zhulin	2	3	2	3	2	3	1	1	3
Torvill, Dean	3	2	3	2	3	2	2	2	2
Gritschuk, Platov	1	1	1	1	1	1	3	3	1

Clearly and conclusively Gritschuk and Platov won the free dance, but the runner-up (crucial, of course, to the overall Championship) turned on who held most second places or better. Torvill and Dean had six, Usova and Zhulin five.

The difficult bit to ingest is that phrase *most second places or better*. You might imagine that in such a tie-break Usova and Zhulin's tally — three second places, two *firsts* — would take precedence over Torvill and Dean, who had the six second places but no firsts at all. But under the rules, first and second places counted just the same in the tie-break: hence 6-5 to Torvill and Dean.

In one way it was satisfactory for them, in another way worrying and inconclusive. They'd return to Milton Keynes and perform major surgery, time running hard against them. They had a few days short of a month before Lillehammer. No-one could have guessed the global furore their performance would detonate.

6

Career Statistics

Jayne Torvill born Nottingham, 7 October 1957. Started skating aged nine.
Christopher Dean born Nottingham, 27 July 1958. Started skating aged 10.

1970 Torvill won the British Junior Pairs Championships with Michael Hutchinson; they were second in the Senior Pairs.

1971 Torvill won the Senior Pairs with Hutchinson.

1972 Dean won the British Primary Dance Championships with Sandra Elson. Torvill and Hutchinson finished 18th in the European Pairs Championships, Gothenburg; second in the British.

1973 Hutchinson left Torvill to find a better partner.

1974 Dean and Elson won the British Junior Dance Championship; sixth in the Seniors.

1975 Elson left to find a better partner; a new Nottingham coach Janet Sawbridge put Torvill and Dean together; they agreed to a month's trial.

1976 Torvill and Dean won the Sheffield Trophy; the Northern Championship; and a summer competition at St. Gervais, France; second at Oberstdorf, Bavaria; fourth at British Championships.

1977 Won Oberstdorf; third in the British Championships.

1978 Ninth in their first European Championships, Strasbourg, eleventh in the World Championships, Ottawa. Sawbridge, married and expecting her first baby, retired. Betty Callaway became their new coach. They agreed to a month's trial with her. Won the John Davis Trophy; and the British Championships (received their first 6.0).

1979 Sixth in the European Championships, Zagreb, eighth in the Worlds, Vienna; won the British Championships; second in Rotary Watches Competition, Richmond; second in the NHK Competition, Tokyo.

1980   Fourth in the Europeans, Gothenburg; fifth in the Olympic Games, Lake Placid; fourth in the Worlds, Dortmund; won the British Championships, and the St. Ivel, Richmond.

1981   Won the Europeans, Innsbruck; the Worlds at Hartford, Connecticut; the British Championships; and the St. Ivel. Awarded the MBE.

1982   Won the Europeans, Lyons; the Worlds, Copenhagen, with *Mack and Mabel;* and the British Championships.

1983   Missed the Europeans, Dortmund (Torvill injured); won the Worlds, Helsinki, with *Barnum*, (nine 6.os for artistic impression in the free); won the British Championships.

1984   Won the European Championships, Budapest; the Olympics, Sarajevo (nine 6.os for artistic impression); and the Worlds, Ottawa, with *Bolero*.

1985   Turned professional, making their first world tour; won the World Professional Championships.

1986   Made their first television special, *Fire and Ice*.

1987   Toured as guests of the American company IceCapades.

1988   Made their second world tour with a company of Soviet skaters.

1990   Won the World Professional Championships. Jayne Torvill married Phil Christensen, a sound engineer with Genesis.

1991   Toured Australia as guests of the South Australian Government. Dean choreographed the programme for French-Canadians Isabelle and Paul Duchesnay, who won the World Championships. Christopher Dean married Isabelle Duchesnay.

1993   Toured the United States and, following a change in Olympic rules, applied to become amateurs again. Christopher and Isabelle divorced.

1994   Won the British Championships at Sheffield with *Face The Music And Dance* (nine 6.os for artistic impression in the free); won the Europeans, Copenhagen, on a count-back tie-break; won bronze in the Winter Olympics, Lillehammer.